The Paris of Appalachia

Pittsburgh in the Twenty-first Century

The Paris of Appalachia

Pittsburgh in the Twenty-first Century

Brian O'Neill

Carnegie Mellon University Press
Pittsburgh 2009

Cover painting by Ron Donoughe
Pittview Ave Vista, oil on panel, 8 x 10 inches, 2001
Collection, Brian O'Neill
www.donoughe.com

Book and cover design: Shahnaz Islam

Library of Congress Control Number 2008940121
ISBN 978-0-88748-509-1
Copyright © 2009 by Brian O'Neill
All rights reserved
Printed and bound in the United States of America

10 9 8 7 6 5 4

for Betsy, Curran and Clare

Contents

Preface

I began this book years ago, before Americans became familiar with phrases like "toxic assets" and "foreclosure tsunami." As the cataclysmic financial events of 2008 and 2009 unfolded, as the nation's wealth vaporized, we in Pittsburgh found ourselves in the unfamiliar position of holding fairly steady.

Don't get that wrong. We will suffer, too. There have been layoffs. Our pension funds imploded with everyone else's. But because Pittsburgh didn't have the population pressure in the past few decades to goose home prices skyward, we didn't have the real estate crash that so many other American places endured. As the joke here went, "you can't get the hangover if you were never at the party."

So even as we prepare for hard times and read of the troubles in Sun Belt communities and in Michigan and Ohio, there has been a bit of a "been there, done that" feeling hereabouts. With the rest of the country, in effect, falling back to meet us, people may be reading this book in a different way than I expected when I began. We are now in such uncertain times, I can't know how the nation will look when you hold this in your hands. But I do know Pittsburgh has come through tougher times. There's comfort in that, and, odd as it sounds, it's possible the rest of the country can learn something from us. If the following isn't a hopeful story, I've done something wrong.

Map of Pittsburgh and Allegheny County. Some of the 90 city neighborhoods and 130 municipalities in Allegheny County. A fuller map would take a bigger book.

The Paris of Appalachia

R on Donoughe is a vista collector. He paints landscapes every day, from hilltops hither and yon. As I ride shotgun in his truck from his studio in Lawrenceville to a hilltop in Reserve, the November sky is overcast. Doesn't matter.

"I've started to really embrace these kinds of days because it makes you feel a certain way," he says as we cross the 40th Street Bridge.

It makes you feel like you're in Pittsburgh, that's for sure. We cross the Allegheny and soon I'm on a road I've never traveled, Logan Street in Millvale, a hill that soars higher than the scalpers' markup outside Heinz Field.

"Pittsburgh is a painter's paradise," Donoughe says. "There's so much variety and texture."

Soon enough we pull over in a quiet slice of inner suburbia, Pittview Avenue. It's a weekday afternoon. Kids are walking home from school. The moisture has made the afternoon blue-gray or maybe blue-violet. Donoughe is interested in how colors change over distance, and we have come to a place where that plays out.

He breaks out his easel, oil paints and an eight-by-ten-inch birch panel. Then he puts on his wide-brimmed hat. Stepping over a guard rail, he sets himself up on a bluff facing the city. The skyline is a couple of milky miles to the southwest. In the middle distance are the homes of Troy Hill, reminiscent now of a model railroad set. A brown hillside slopes down from our right to our left, and a handful of evergreens frame a red and white house just a few hundred yards ahead.

The scene is not so much pretty as it is stunning. Donoughe has painted on and off here for a couple of years, yet, with the changing light and weather and seasons, he never sees the same place twice.

About this time, a truck stops behind us. A worker who is carting a couple of road-kill deer to who-knows-where tells Donoughe he's painting "a masterpiece." Then the man drives on.

"Sometimes I think I'm responding to the way Pittsburgh feels as much as the way it looks."

It took this country boy from Cambria County five or ten years to warm up to Pittsburgh, but once he digested what the city was all about, it became his constant muse. I know how that feels.

A city with heft—that's how a friend who moved here from Colorado described Pittsburgh. You sense it as you walk the quirky Downtown street grid that must have made more sense when a military surveyor sketched it out on parchment in 1784. Or you drive, for the thousandth time, past rusted iron railings and crumbling walls that have not a savior in sight.

Think Houston in the 1970s or Seattle in the 1990s, then throw them together and you'll have a sense of the head of steam Pittsburgh had going a century ago. Pittsburgh grew from 78,000 in 1860 to nearly 670,000 in 1930. That was a good time to grow rich. Many did on the sweat of tens of thousands more. Victorian wealth remains evident in our architecture, our culture, our foundations, our hospitals and our universities. We have the usual love-hate relationship with Old Money here, maybe even an advanced case, but when Pittsburgh went reeling into the post-industrial age, Old Money helped break its fall.

New Money is what we lack. The city is down to roughly the same population it had in the 1890s, and Allegheny County is hovering around its 1920s numbers. Pittsburghers are dying faster than they're being born, but our hometown still has great bones. The smoke has cleared to reveal stunning green hillsides, and our rivers have been freed from centuries in an industrial headlock. Spectacular vistas are so commonplace none of us will ever get to them all. Our generation's principal task is to keep all worth keeping. That's not much of a chore when compared to our ancestors' capacity for innovation.

Yet we're failing, which drives me nuts.

What I hope to do in this book is encourage a discussion of how city and mill town and suburb might work together so everyone thrives. Most of us can point to development that has been detrimental to both city and suburban life, even as the fragmentation of Allegheny County fosters an us-versus-them mentality within the region while the rest of America eats our lunch.

We need a new conservatism willing to conserve, a new liberalism to stoke the embers of egalitarianism in the Pennsylvania cities where our nation was born. The intense media focus on the city's woes obscures the greater problem. The entire region's population declined 10 percent during the 1990s while the nation grew by 13 percent. It kept shrinking in the first decade of the new century, losing more people than any metropolis other than New Orleans, which had a flood you might have read about it.

Yet the *Places Rated Almanac* has decided twice in the past twenty-two years that Pittsburgh is America's "Most Livable City." Given the all too easy jokes about it also being "most leaveable," what's up with this place?

"The Paris of Appalachia" some have called Pittsburgh derisively, because it's still the largest city along this gorgeous mountain chain that needs a better press agent. I've long felt we should embrace that title, though few are with me. Several tried to talk me out of slapping it on the cover, but were we called "The Paris of the Rockies," we wouldn't run from it. Sometimes we're so afraid of what others think, we're afraid to say who we are. This city is not Midwestern. It's not East Coast. It's just Pittsburgh, and there's no place like it.

That's both its blessing and its curse.

Steeltown Blues

When I arrived in Pittsburgh in the fall of 1988, the region had every right to be in the late stages of trauma. Nearly one hundred thirty thousand manufacturing jobs, half of them in steel, had been lost in less than ten years, and the city's beloved thrice-elected mayor, Richard Caliguiri, had died in office that spring, teaching his people a new word they'd rather not have learned, the rare disease that killed him at fifty-six, amyloidosis.

Yet in that same decade, the skyline had been juiced with what the locals immodestly called "Renaissance II." (Europe, meantime, still claims only one.) Jobs in retail, trade, finance and services grew by more than seventy-five thousand. And the first "Most Livable" designation came.

So, rather than negativity, what I mostly found when I unpacked and settled into a Shadyside apartment was a we-can-fix-this spirit that would make Frank Capra blush.

That year the people of McKeesport, with the help of a local bank, raised more than one hundred thousand dollars in a week's time to keep cops on the beat. The leaders of West Homestead played the lottery with the long-shot hope of filling a cavernous hole in the budget. (Didn't happen.) The governments in Homestead and Lincoln were looking for handouts, and getting them, from local businesses. These were Band-Aids, not cures, but with the stunned giants along the rivers no longer producing smoke or paychecks, the traditions and rhythms of home and neighborhood cushioned the blows.

Nobody I met in my early days here exemplifed that resilience better than LaMonte Pruitt, who went from a South High School basketball hero to a small college all-star, to a couple of years as a minor-league basketball player in Scranton. Then, in the mid-'70s, he hooked up with the Union Railroad as a brakeman. Life was good. We're talking thirty grand a year, a fancy crib in West Mifflin, a new Cadillac every other year and plenty of weekends in New York.

Then he woke up one day and he saw his '82 Fleetwood—"chocolate brown, chocolate brown-leather seats, maxed out—you couldn't hear the engine if you were standing next to it"—gone. The repo man had driven his baby away.

"It was like a little kid seeing that his puppy got run over."

Pruitt's glory days seemed to end with the railroad's. USX wasn't bringing his brakeman's job back. He'd go three years without work. He'd go on welfare. He'd see old railroad friends hit skid row. He says two even wound up floating in the Monongahela.

Pruitt didn't have much to sell. He hadn't gotten a degree from Lincoln University in Missouri, opting instead for a shot at pro basketball in 1974, an effort that went around the rim and out when he was injured after a couple of exhibition games with the Seattle Supersonics. But this guy led his collegiate basketball conference in rebounding two years in a row. There could be no tougher rebound than the one he'd have to make in Pittsburgh.

His biggest fan, his mom, Virginia Poindexter, never lost confidence in him. And his stepfather, Herschel Poindexter, who raised six children on the money he brought home from the Homestead Works, had always told him, "If it's good honest work, don't ever be ashamed of it."

So Pruitt started shining shoes. He didn't broadcast it. "Some people look at it as a black stereotype thing." But around 1985, he began working in the basement of what was then the tallest building between New York and Chicago. (A city that can't get out of neutral makes its claims in the past tense, with qualifiers.) Pruitt became a fixture in Ed Vavro's barber shop in the USX Tower. When acquaintances asked him where he worked, he'd say "The Steel Building" and leave it at that.

"It got me back on my feet," Pruitt said. "Slow money beats no money."

Wearing a shirt and tie and charging a buck a pair, he never had a down day. Just ask Vavro. Pruitt would talk sports, make friends and, eventually, make his rebounds.

Through someone he met at the shop, Pruitt was introduced to an old cobbler who convinced him that the big money in shoes was on the bottoms. With a year of classes at South High in shoe repair behind him, Pruitt, at thirty-nine, landed a job at Victor's Shoe and Luggage Repair on a side street between Fifth and Forbes in Oakland. For a while you could

LaMonte Pruitt. Photo by Larry Rippel.

see a six-foot-six man hunkering under a six-foot-three ceiling, stitching boots, cutting soles and tapping heels.

I met him in there one day and the laughs came easily on both sides of the counter as customers came in and out, but there weren't enough of them. Shoe repair turned out to be another dying industry. The new soft shoe is not a sweet song to a cobbler. Pruitt had to go back to shining shoes, at Pittsburgh International Airport, in the early 1990s.

So why is Pruitt driving a new car again?

In 1995, he was called back to work at the Union Railroad.

"Of course," he said, "I ran with both feet."

By 2001, he was promoted to conductor, boss of the train. That goes back to something he'd told me, more than a decade before. Pruitt's other game is chess, you see.

"When you get your queen taken, most guys are humiliated into quitting. When the queen's gone, the king feels just about like abdicating."

Sometimes, though, after the other guy has lifted most of your pieces, you find yourself in exactly the right square. Rebounding is all about positioning, no matter what the game. I have reason to hope that Pittsburgh is in that square right now. The queen, the industry that defined us, is all but gone. So, it seems, is that confidence I encountered in the late 1980s. Seeing the city's credit rating tank to junk bond status for more than a year can do that to a people. But we're a long way from dead.

In her 1998 book-length valentine to Pittsburgh, *Singing the City*, Laurie Graham wrote, "For the rest of the nation this city has been a place apart and we know it."

Graham was wary of losing our central story, our steel heritage, which "provides a sense of who we are." While that's true even for those, such as I, who never set foot in a mill until it was time to write its obituary, Graham's fears are misplaced. The irony of our times is that we have to scrap the current governmental structure, as so many steel mills were scrapped, to conserve our legacy, but I don't see Pittsburgh losing its defining story.

Steel remains everywhere we look. Steel is celebrated in our bridges, in the murals of our churches and courthouses and subway stations, and most especially on the sides of football helmets. Steelworkers will be remembered when every Pittsburgher now living is gone. Steel is our bone structure. Our problem is the flesh is weak.

It's natural to glory in our past. Most American cities have yet to see their finest architecture, their highest population, their greatest impact on the world. We in Pittsburgh almost certainly have. We used to be a much bigger deal, and we stopped being one just as our country became the most dominant one in the history of the Earth. We get little immigration at a time when that's about all some Americans can talk about. Sometimes, to borrow the phrase of a woman I met when Pittsburgh was new to me, we can feel like a shrinking party balloon that's been stuck too long to the wall.

Yet, if we'd care to admit it, most of us also find ourselves more fortunate than our ancestors, with cleaner air and water, less crowded homes, better working conditions, more stuff. Is that dissonance holding us back? Does it leave us with fewer risk-takers and more complacency?

Scattered among us remain these optimists. They are either resilient visionaries or hopeless fantasists, depending on your point of view, but, on my best days, I throw in with the visionaries.

"We agonize over our Downtown," complains native son Dejan Kovacevic, who covers the Pirates for the *Post-Gazette* and whose love of the city oozes from his keyboard. "But we have two bad streets out of thirty.

And most of the other twenty-eight are better now than they were five years ago. We agonize over our taxes—which are awful—but never compare our cost of living and ability to choose where we wish to live with a place like San Francisco, where both are impossible."

Actually, some of us do that comparison. When the Steelers faced the Seattle Seahawks in the 2006 Super Bowl, my brother-in-law in Seattle mailed us a clip from his local paper. Headlined "Seattle vs. Pittsburgh," it offered photos of two $550,000 houses, one in each city. The Seattle house was a 2,000 square foot, three-bedroom bungalow. The Pittsburgh house was a six-bedroom, five-fireplace, 4,650 square foot Tudor mansion in our East End.

Some days, when I'm getting down about Pittsburgh or my lot in life or the Pirates' need for a left-handed power hitter, I go to another city's Web site and check the real estate prices. Most of them allow you to specify the size of the house you seek. I hit sites for San Francisco, New York or Boston and punch in the dimensions of our nineteenth-century rowhouse on the North Side. Suddenly my net worth quintuples and I sign off, feeling like Donald Trump with a more sensible haircut.

The Third Bear

Riverfronts freed from an industrial headlock: Kristen Serrano of Lawrenceville plays frisbee on the North Shore in 2007. John Heller, Pittsburgh Post-Gazette.

I should tell you how I got here. I used to live, spent almost a decade in fact, in a sweet place called Roanoke, Virginia, a little city about two hundred miles due south that is likewise snuggled in the foothills of Appalachia. Roanoke's easy pace suited me, as did the housing prices, but I missed the buzz of my native New York. I'd grown up on Long Island and, like two of my three siblings, didn't want to go back once I made it to the mainland. But I missed big league baseball, corner bars, universities, professional theater, competing newspapers, Italians, Poles and people who considered St. Patrick's Day a legitimate holiday. It was my great fortune to find Pittsburgh about halfway between Roanoke and New York, not just on the map, but in personality. I had stumbled upon the third bear of cities. Not too big. Not too small. Just right.

My first winter in town, the January 9 issue of *The New Yorker* magazine was hard to find in the Golden Triangle, mostly because critic Brendan Gill, the epitome of seen-it-all New York sophistication, made this mind-blowing statement:

> *If Pittsburgh were situated somewhere in the heart of Europe, tourists would eagerly journey hundreds of miles out of their way to visit it.*

Gill saw the city's steep population decline as a blessing. He thought our numbers then (nearly three hundred seventy thousand people, or about sixty thousand more folks than there are today) were probably ideal for a late twentieth-century city.

"In this period of feverish gigantism," Gill asked, "can cities as small as I would like them to be prove themselves capable of surviving and prospering?"

That is the big question of this book, but first we need to broaden Gill's concept of Pittsburgh, and maybe ours, too.

As anyone who has lived here for more than a half-hour can tell you, the real Pittsburgh is not confined by the city limits. One of every four jobs in the seven-county area is within three miles of the Point,[1] but most of those paychecks are spent in the malls and superstores of the suburbs. The city is a political construct left over from the horse-and-buggy era. The real Pittsburgh stretches from Peters through Cranberry, from Murrysville through Hopewell, and to points beyond.

I learned almost immediately that my move to the city proper was based in part on an assumption no one else shared. I thought that the new columnist for *The Pittsburgh Press* was expected to live in the city, not the suburbs. Then I came to work and discovered that pretty much the entire editorial board lived in Mt. Lebanon. Nobody gave a tinker's damn where the columnist lived, because the true Pittsburgh, the culture of Pittsburgh, is not restricted by the political boundaries.

By the time I realized this, it didn't matter. I was not so much stuck in the city as stuck *on* the city.

View of the Clemente Bridge from the North Side. Darrel Sapp, Pittsburgh Post-Gazette.

Lawrenceville

I was single when I moved here and, one hot Saturday afternoon, I dropped off a friend in Lawrenceville, and started doing the one-way street shuffle, taking the long way round to Penn Avenue, when I saw this sign at the corner of Forty-fifth and Davison, "Freddie's."

I have a theory on neighborhood bars. The more field research I do, the truer it seems. Put simply, the farther from the main drag, the better the bar, because it has to be to survive.

I pulled over and walked into the coolness of the place with a copy of the afternoon paper. (That should tell you this was a while ago.) A handful of guys were in the back tossing darts. I took a seat at the bar for a cold Iron draft.

The bartender and the guy to my left were teetering on the brink of an argument. It was your classic barroom debate, just a couple of Joes disagreeing on the difference between the French and American Revolutions.

Larry, behind the bar, was trying to get a word in with Len, who was working on a wine cooler (I told you this was a while ago) and a passion for history. Len was arguing that The American Revolution couldn't be seen as a radical movement at all; it was a movement that began when colonists sought to recover their traditional rights as Englishmen.

Larry was saying, sure, but it was still a revolution, in fact the only one in history that truly succeeded because it was based on economic and personal liberties.

I pretended to read the baseball box scores, but who could concentrate? If I hear one more argument about the relative value of eighteenth-century revolutions in a bar, that'll make two. So I decided to do what I always do when I'm in over my head: channel Cliff Clavin, the know-it-all on *Cheers*.

"Yeah, well what about Tom Paine?" I said to Len, bringing up an important radical writer of the American Revolution whose extensive writing had barely gotten my cursory glance. "He surely was a radical . . . ."

"Well, Tom Paine," Len began, and was off, taking us with him. Soon we were fighting the French and Indian War, a world war that George Washington set off only a half-hour's drive south, which was enough to bring the other bartender swooping in. Craig is just another one of those guys who can't get over the injustice of Colonel Henry Bouquet not getting his due for defeating an unknown number of Delawares, Shawnees, Mingos and Wyandots twenty-five miles down the road at Bushy Run in the summer of 1763.

By the time Len mentioned Bouquet's copy of Caesar's commentaries on the Gallic Wars, his blueprint for bringing civilized warfare into barbarian territory, I was confident this was the damnedest bar I'd ever breached, and my study had been extensive. I said as much, too. What could precipitate a brawl in Freddie's? Did people crack heads over the strategies at Fort Duquesne?

I had them pegged for graduate students or professors from the University of Pittsburgh or Carnegie Mellon University, both ten minutes away. Your average American just doesn't steep himself in history this way. All generalists are dead or at *Jeopardy* auditions. You simply don't find them in the wild.

But the only credential these guys offered was a natural curiosity. Larry Granberg owned the bar. Craig was his younger brother. Len Lloyd was a draftsman. Speaking of drafts, I had another.

I soon was calling my friend and telling her the movie could wait. She had to see this place first. She came in just as the conversation hovered over the differences between Jeffersonian democracy and Marxism. The bar began filling up and the Pirates game came on and fizzled out and we never did go see *When Harry Met Sally* . . . .

Freddie's changed hands on St. Patrick's Day 1999 and became Kelly's Korner, but I bring up the old, debate-happy crowd here because theirs is the kind of conversation we need to have. Only we need to be talking about what's been happening, and not happening, in America for the past half-century. Much as I love Pittsburgh, we're more than a tad insular here, better at knowing the old days than what's over that next hill. You can't swing a cat Downtown without hitting someone who can give you ten minutes on Andy Carnegie or Andy Warhol, the Homestead Strike or the Homestead Grays. But we're largely unaware of the way things are done in cities that are more successful than, though not nearly as cool as, ours.

Wait on that thought just a second while we have a bite to eat with the Condelucis. Theirs is the kind of story Pittsburgh doesn't want to lose as it moves forward.

Overlooking "The Rocks"

Condeluci Hill is our city in miniature. To have dinner with the Condelucis in their neighborhood cabana, on a hill overlooking McKees Rocks, is to enter into about sixty years of unbroken love. Even in Western Pennsylvania, where tight families are nearly as common as Sunday dinners, nothing matches this family compound.

Until the spring of 2006 when a house sold to someone outside the family, only Condeluci blood relatives lived on this hill. There are eleven related families, four of which live in bungalows built by the Condelucis themselves. Almost every night, family members gather for coffee in the cabana the Condeluci brothers built more than forty years ago beside Gento Pool, which they also built and named for their late parents, Generina and Antonio Condeluci.

"You put cement in an Italian's hands and he goes wild," Sinbad Condeluci told me modestly on a night long ago.

It was Sinbad and his brother, Sam, who struck a handshake deal with a McKees Rocks doctor to buy the three and one-half-acre hill in 1944. There long was a pact to sell or will the homes only to family, and now a fourth generation of Condeluci children plays in the woods behind the

Frank Condeluci enjoys a toast as his wife Gloria, left, joins him and several generations in the cabana on Condeluci Hill in 1989. Photo by Bill Wade for The Pittsburgh Press. *Courtesy of the* Pittsburgh Post-Gazette.

homes, on the same grounds their great-grandparents explored as children.

You have to go back to the great-grandparents to understand. Generina and Antonio had nine children, five boys and four girls, who grew up at the foot of this hill. If you're lucky enough to be invited to the cabana for spaghetti, homemade sausage and wine, generations of Condelucis look over your shoulder from the photos lining the long dining room.

Betty, a middle child among the original nine, recalled her mom's advice. Make yourself a little piece of bread with butter and eat it before your man comes home. If you fight and don't get around to dinner, at least you won't be hungry.

"My father said you'll all marry women from different nationalities," Sinbad said. "They'll fight. You must never fight."

The brothers performed as predicted, marrying Jewish, Slovak, Italian and Ukranian women, and the boys never fought amongst themselves. Jane said she didn't talk to her brother-in-law Sam for two years, but that never stopped her Sinbad from talking with his brother.

That brings us to the question all outsiders have. How is it for those who marry into this family?

Gloria, Frank's wife, said she was intimidated when she arrived. Now, thinking of the next generations, she said, "It's a shame the hill isn't bigger."

Later that night, after the Condelucis scattered down the block to flip on a TV or get ready for bed, I was at the split-level on the corner with a postcard-perfect view of the Golden Triangle, five miles off. Al, Sinbad's son and a father of three himself, told me how it was for him. He travels on the job, and when he explains where he lives, he hears: "Are you kidding me? In America in . . . [Fill in any year here. Al has been hearing this question for decades.]?"

"I know it sounds idyllic," he says, "and it is."

As I said, I like to think of Condeluci Hill as Pittsburgh writ small, but the hill has done a better job of attracting newcomers than the region has during the past half-century. If you get Pittsburgh, and not everyone does, it's going to give back well more than you put into it. But you have to understand one crucial aspect of Pittsburghers going in. They have a formidable, largely unspoken solidarity that can come only from generations lived through the best and worst of times. People are very resistant to change here.

How many Pittsburghers does it take to change a light bulb?

Two. One to change the bulb and one to talk about how good the old one was. (In my neighborhood, they'll also research its ancestry.)

North Side

I was walking back from a neighbor's Twelfth Night dessert party. When you live in and among restored nineteenth-century rowhouses, the older the reason to party, the better. Anyway, I was buzzing on a sugar high. If there can be such a thing as a freeloader getting his money's worth, I'd done it, shuffling along Linda Ianotta's dessert table like a kleptomaniac holed up in a bakery. Ianotta bakes the way Pavarotti sang.

I was within a hundred steps of my house when a big guy in overalls, walking the opposite way on Galveston Avenue, stopped short and yelled over:

"You the writer?"

I was wondering if I should plead guilty. Had I written anything lately against men wearing overalls? I mentally reviewed my recent efforts. Though I nearly dozed off, I did determine that my columns had been overall-free.

"Yessir," I answered warily.

The man smiled and said he'd wanted to meet me. I walked over and shook his hand. He said I needed to come over to his friend's apartment, off the alley behind my house, and have a beer with his one and only and their friends.

There may be men who would turn their backs on such an offer. But freeloading, I feel, is no part-time gig. If you want to call yourself a plunderer, you must give it your all.

So I walked into a kitchen in mid-party. Rum, Kool-Aid and beer were on the table, and four people were around it. I was introduced to a crowd with North Side roots. Everyone there was pretty good about accepting me, despite my being there only one and a half years at that time. They did have it in for all these yuppies moving in, but if they thought I fit the description, they let me slide. Maybe it was the way I drank my high-test Kool-Aid.

These folks had a different perspective on the street I thought I knew. They were down on neighborhood leaders for forcing the rough-and-tumble Hob Nob saloon to shut down a few years before. The Allegheny West Civic Council saw it as a nuisance, but one person's nuisance is another's solace. This crowd once loafed there.

And then Tim Bartins, the guy in overalls, asked what I was going to say about Sears closing in Allegheny Center Mall.

I told him I'd been writing too much about the North Side lately.

If you count the North Side as one neighborhood, Bartins reminded me, it's the biggest one this shrinking city has. He had sold Christmas trees each December in the parking lot across from Sears, and a closing would affect him directly. But this wasn't about him.

He likened the shoppers who drove out of the city for the Sears at Ross Park Mall to people driving Japanese cars. They were killing the local economy.

Yes, but both the Japanese and the North Hills have given middle-class consumers what they want: something they feel they can depend on. I had frequented the Sears at the Incredible Shrinking Mall, and shopping there could make you feel like Will Smith in *I Am Legend*. Everyone else had vanished.

I can afford to laugh about it, but more than a third of city households don't have access to a car. Half the black families in town don't. The draining of the city's retail options isn't so funny if you're walking or waiting in the sun or snow for the bus.

The day after this Kool-Aid party, I dug through the newspaper clipping file to find the story of this mall. The hyper-optimistic predictions made by urban planners of the 1950s and 1960s were anti-prophetic. In October 1961, a story in *The Pittsburgh Press* began:

"Allegheny Center, the $85 million renewal of the North Side's business district, will open the city's offensive to regain people lost to the suburbs."

The offensive was no more successful than the one the Argentines launched in the Falkland Islands War. The old mall is now living a second life as an office park, a dimly lit place I sometimes pass through because it sits astride the North Side's major east-west crossroads, Federal and Ohio Streets. The center has had some mild success in this reincarnation, but even that is slipping, and the office work there always has been an island unto itself, cut off from the neighborhoods surrounding it. Allegheny Center can't keep much more retail commerce than a coffee kiosk and a shoe repair going. So the real effect of the 1950s plan has been to rip the heart out of old Allegheny's historic downtown, making the comeback of the surrounding neighborhoods all the more remarkable.

The hundreds of restored Victorian homes in the Mexican War Streets, the most famous of the city's neighborhood renewals, weren't supposed to survive. These 1950s planners wanted to level every one and build high rises like those in Allegheny Center. Those apartments retain appeal—it can cost roughly $1,200 a month for a two-bedroom plus parking there—but they'll never play the dominating role that planners envisioned back when.

Tens of thousands of us have hung on, sometimes in spite of, sometimes because of, grand plans for urban renewal. Some have moved—or been moved—and others have taken their places. On any given night, the diversity that is both the North Side's strength and its flash point may reach out and shake a newcomer from his complacency.

Sears split, but I know this is where I'm supposed to be. I bought my first townhouse just about one hundred years after my grandmother got off the boat to work in one much like it. Anna McStay came over from Ireland

The urban playground, where a couple of twenty-first century maidens climb upon the nineteenth-century Stone Maidens *outside the Pittsburgh Children's Museum on the North Side. The sculpture by Eugenio Pedon once stood on the roof of the Old Post Office on Smithfield Street. Photo by Betsy O'Neill.*

the boat to work in one much like it. Anna McStay came over from Ireland as a young girl, joining her older sister in domestic work in Montclair, New Jersey. I believe Grandma would like that I'm here, though she'd be astonished at the Christmas tours the neighborhood puts on each year, with people paying more than she made in a week just to spend a few minutes in these places not touching anything.

I'm pretty much back in the life that my father had as a boy in the Bronx when the twentieth century was young, the one he told us about at the dinner table, and made sure his children did not have after we joined the great migration to the suburbs after World War II. Dad could not have realized how those dinnertime tales would leave their mark.

I loved my father, born in 1910, a very gentle, warm-hearted guy who didn't become a father until he was forty-three. (I would follow his pattern closely, becoming a father the month I turned forty-two). But the Bronx that Dad spoke about, where he ran errands around the corner for his mom and played sandlot ball with my uncles, was nothing like the Bronx we'd see on trips to Yankee Stadium. In the 1970s, the Bronx was burning.

It wasn't until I moved to Pittsburgh that I got it. This was city life Dad must have known. This was that rare metropolis you could put your arms around.

When my brother, sisters and I were kids, Dad read us books about young men going out to seek their fortune. He'd be surprised where I found mine. They're not making places like my neighborhood anymore, though new urbanists are trying. Pittsburgh is a gift my wife and I can leave our children, if it doesn't kill itself first.

Town

When I grew up in suburban New York, we called Manhattan "The City." Even New Yorkers in the outer boroughs of Queens and Staten Island call Manhattan "The City." Suburbanites outside San Francisco do the same thing.

We don't do that in Pittsburgh. We have an entirely different way of thinking about our center of civic gravity. Old-timers call Downtown simply "Town," as in "We live close to Town" or "When we go to Town . . . ." I like the comfort level and sense of ownership in those phrases. Nobody but brochure writers or journalists calls the heart of the region "The Golden Triangle." It's "Town."

I'm not saying that's unique to Pittsburgh. "Going to town" is all-American slang for having yourself a time. But New Yorkers I've brought to Town are struck by certain things. My childhood buddy, Joe LoCurto, couldn't believe our little subway. "It's free?" he asked incredulously. My little brother, The Incredible Dullboy, who came here for a job interview in the late 1980s before finally deciding to make a fortune on Long Island by selling penile implants (a story for another book) was stunned by the casual kindness of natives. All he had to do was look as if he was trying to find an address Downtown and a person would walk up to help him. New Yorkers are more caring than legend has them, but they don't do that.

Dullboy, who is anything but, also was taken aback by the friendliness outside Town. I was showing him and his wife, Jennifer, around the North

Clare and Curran O'Neill play amid the water jets at the PPG Place fountain, which morphs into a skating rink each winter. Photo by Betsy O'Neill.

Hills for possible places to live, and when we drove into a subdivision, a guy driving the other way waved.

After I waved back, my brother asked, "You know that guy?"

"No," I said, "He was just being friendly."

"Just being friendly?" Dullboy asked.

"Yeah," I said.

"What is this?" he demanded. "I'm a human being. You're a human being. Now I gotta wave to ya? I can't live here. That's messed up."

No, it's Pittsburgh. We're not really a city; we just play one on TV. We're a big Town, almost all of us ready to embrace our inner rube. We marvel at fireworks no matter how many times we see them, a truth that George Romero used as the sly inside joke in his 2005 zombie flick, *Land of the Dead*. Sean Cannon, writer for the Pittsburgh-spoofing Web site, Carbolic Smoke Ball, says, "If they offered proctology exams followed by fireworks, Pittsburghers would go."

Then there's Light Up Night, where tens of thousands swarm Downtown, the one place they can be assured of not taking in the full vista of all

We blow off a lot of fireworks. Tony Tye, Pittsburgh Post-Gazette.

those sparkling skyscrapers.

We do these things because Town is our common ground. When the nation's courts decided in the 1980s that government-sponsored manger scenes were a no-no at Christmas, Joseph and Mary came to town anyway, hopping out of a gray Mazda GLC and arranging themselves in front of the City-County Building. They were Sue Beneditti of Elizabeth Township and Steven A. Spates of Wilkinsburg, costumed members of the Word and Worship Fellowship Church in North Braddock. It was a beautiful, peaceful protest, which made me even more grateful for a government that could separate church from state and allow Christians to show up with an unsanitized, commercial-free, straight-from-the-heart-and-not-from-Caesar celebration of the holiday.

I was new to Town then, and noticed that that these people did not reside in the city. That does not mean Town does not belong to them, equally, or is not crucial to their identity as Pittsburghers.

Town has fallen on hard times. The Cultural District booms but the shopping district reels. I still managed to do nearly all my Christmas shopping in Town in a recent year, but that's a game I have come to call "The December Challenge." Tom Murphy, mayor for a dozen years ending in 2005, was very successful in other parts of town, launching a retail resurgence in East Liberty and razing the old Jones & Laughlin steel mill on the South Side to make way for a popular retail and entertainment complex. But Murphy made huge, disastrous bets on two Downtown department stores, Lazarus and Lord & Taylor, that quickly went the way of the dodo and the prothonotary. The Lazarus building is being revamped as a meld of shops, offices, condos and penthouses, a far smarter bet.

There also has been a boom in high-end high rises in and around Downtown. New apartments where rent begins at $1,900 a month and condos selling for $200 thousand to $1.8 million overlook the Monongahela River and the Allegheny, on Fort Pitt and Fort Duquesne boulevards, respectively. Just upriver, the old Heinz plant and the Armstrong Cork factory flank the Allegheny with competing loft space. This town always has taken its own sweet time; yuppies elsewhere in America learned to nail wall hangings to exposed brick back in the Reagan Era. Still, our Downtown was actually one of twelve in America that grew while the city surrounding it shrank during the 1990s.[2] So what if we cheated a little by sticking in the new Allegheny County Jail? We've got water, we've got space, and these close-in condos look a lot better when gasoline bounces between two and four dollars a gallon.

"This is not revitalization," Dejan Kovacevic insists, "only because the prefix 're-' is incorrect. No one ever lived Downtown, not even when the city topped six hundred thousand. This is all new. We have no idea where this will lead us, but it cannot be a negative to have the core getting filled. Not for our culture, businesses, recreation, anything. But we agonize over Lord & Taylor closing thirty-two stores simultaneously and one of them being ours."

Dejan exaggerates when he says nobody ever lived Downtown. Frenchmen threw their sleeping bags down at Fort Duquesne more than two hundred fifty years ago, and North Side neighborhood legend has it that our Irishmen used to fight the Point's Irishmen on the Allegheny River bridges for sport. Davey Lawrence, the New Deal Democratic boss and post-war mayor, grew up on the Point, and ordered his own boyhood neighborhood leveled in the 1950s to make way for Gateway Center and Point State Park.

Dejan himself was born to this new Golden Triangle, spending his toddling years in a Washington Plaza apartment and another one across from the old Horne's building on Stanwix, before his family moved to Monroeville when he was in the third grade. But you get his drift: The city is not as far adrift as some think. Someday soon, an empty nester or striving young lawyer with a swank address in Town will discover, as I have, the joy of Weldin's, the stationery store on Wood Street that is always a-clutter, with a dog and a cat beside this counter or that, and staffed by women possessing the graciousness, temperament and pace of a less harried era. It's been around since 1852; it's in an old bank building with a balcony now; and going there for our Christmas stationery has become a December rite for me. Weldin's reminds me that I live in a real place and not just another exit off an Interstate.

Despite such throwbacks that retain their niche, Town could no more beat the suburbs at shopping today than it could at golf. To which one can only say, so what? So what if shoppers go to suburban malls or the city's Eastside or SouthSide Works now? We have to figure out what people want from Town in the twenty-first century and concentrate on that. It's clear it's still a prime destination or the city couldn't get a quarter for every seven and half minutes somebody wants to park at a meter. The current strategy, adding housing and treating it more like a neighborhood, is Town's best hope in decades. We have to remember that what some of us love about Town is an idealized image, informed and fueled by those epic black-and-white photographs from the first couple of thirds of the twentieth century that are forever playing the Carnegie Museum of Art. Town was never all that poetic. No place could be.

Not that there's anything wrong with wanting it be all that. That helps define us, too. I first grasped that truth when I got busy chasing down a memory held by a prematurely nostalgic young woman back in the early 1990s. On a beautiful Indian summer November Friday, I bumped into Kristin Kovacic on a Stanwix Avenue traffic island. Ms. Kovacic, then 28, was with a friend and in mid-lament about the 85-foot Christmas tree climbing the walls of Horne's, which still held its Stanwix-Penn Avenue corner then.

That tree wasn't what she wanted to see the day after Halloween. She reminisced about how much sweeter Christmastimes past were, when people were willing to wait a little.

"I think Pittsburgh is a rare city," she said. "You can have certain kinds of memories that would date you in another city."

Ms. Kovacic grew up in Carrick and is now raising a family in Oakland. She remembered Thanksgiving as the starting gun for the shopping season. She didn't care to see any department store tree go up before the turkey had a chance to go down.

"We always had Thanksgiving dinner at one or two o'clock," she said. "Everyone would pile in a car as soon as it would start to get dark. We would go Downtown to see all the windows."

That meant Kaufmann's, Gimbels and finally Horne's. Kovacic said she always had a keen sense of seeing something brand new, "this image of little elves" working so the windows could be unveiled that evening. After hitting all the stores, the Kovacics and their cousins would head back home to gobble turkey sandwiches, where men watched football in a house where "gravy is a beverage."

By mid-November, the Christmas tree on the old Horne's building in Downtown Pittsburgh is taking shape. Steve Mellon, Pittsburgh Post-Gazette.

Kovacic had made this long-gone Pittsburgh so vivid, I felt its loss. So I called Jacie Thompson at home to ask when Horne's first let the air out of Pittsburgh Thanksgivings.

Ms. Thompson, retired only four weeks then, was special events coordinator for Horne's for thirty years. She listened as I relayed Ms. Kovacic's lament, and then she pointed out something to me. The Christmas windows always have pre-dated Thanksgiving in Pittsburgh. The traditional opening for the shopping season is Light Up Night, more than two weeks before.

"Maybe some parents deliberately didn't tell their children any sooner," Ms. Thompson said. "When you're little, you don't have any sense of time."

I called Ms. Kovacic back and told her she'd been seeing two-week-old displays all those years. I might as well have knocked her in the head with an 85-foot tree.

"That's why I'm a fiction writer," she said. "The truth is so disappointing."

Ah, but to me, that only makes the story sweeter. Think of it. Obviously, the Kovacics, and the dozens of others who came to Town all those special nights, were able to keep Christmas from crossing the Thanksgiving line through sheer force of will.

Gimbels is gone and Horne's went, too. Lazarus, not living up to its namesake, could not rise from the dead. Kaufmann's morphed into Macy's. But it's still our Town. Twenty years from now, when a thirtysomething girl remembers Town, all her spins on the PPG Place ice rink will have been perfect and the fish sandwich she had at the Oyster House will be like none she has tasted since.

Don't Mess with Pittsburgh

Robin Troy, far left, and other residents of Pittsburgh's Deutschtown neighborhood sing away the troublesome. Bob Donaldson, Pittsburgh Post-Gazette.

It's the conceit of this book that a city's story is best told from street level. All of us do something to wag the urban tale and make Pittsburgh matter. Take that time Henrietta Raffaele slapped me, because she had a right. By that I mean both a right hook and a reason.

Nan Horton and I were walking her South Oakland neighborhood on a warm March morning, checking the litter and graffiti, when we came upon Ms. Raffaele sweeping up the alley beside her home. She pointed her broom at a pile of beer bottles, remnants of a St. Patrick's Day/Big

East Championship booze fest in the student ghetto, and said, "That's a disgrace."

She grew up in the neighborhood, so I asked how old she was, and that's when she reached up and gave me a playful slap on my left cheek.

"Write down eighty-two," Ms. Raffaele said. "I'll knock off a couple of years."

I liked her moxie, and I also like that this is a town where that decidedly old-fashioned word fits so many people. Didn't Sophie Masloff, at seventy-three and in her housecoat, chase a pair of burglars down her apartment building stairwell when she was mayor? Didn't the ex-prizefighter, Billy Conn, in his seventies, knock a robber to the ground with one quick left in a Beechwood Boulevard convenience store? Didn't Josephine Slater, eighty-two, of Midland, pull her pistol and chase off a shotgun-wielding robber who came into Josephine's Bar back in '06?

Damned right they did.

John Laundrie has moxie, too. Laundrie, sixty and change, was a little way down the same alley, brushing black paint over a vulgar graffito, a chore he takes up every few months. Let others wait for the city's Graffiti Busters to ride in with their high-pressure cleaning and sanding machines. These two don't dawdle. Oh, and he'd like to hang the culprit by his privates.

"The hell with that slap on the wrist."

"I'd rather pay and get it done," Raffaele said, referring, I believe, to the painting and not the public hanging. "I can't stand slop."

As we walked away that day, Horton, who came to the neighborhood as a University of Pittsburgh student in the mid-1970s and stayed to raise eight children, said, "You have to have that kind of spunk and be that feisty to stay here. You're not going to find any lightweights around here."

It's true. Pittsburgh breeds some wonderfully tough people. Our women often have the kindest souls, might even call you "hon," but bring trouble to their neighborhood and they can be on you like fries in a Primanti Brothers sandwich. Many a street would be lost were it not for its women taking steps June Cleaver never dreamed of.

A few winters back, Robin Troy, a mother of five, and her neighbors did something special in Deutschtown. Their part of the North Side, tucked between the Parkway North and the foot of Troy Hill, had been haunted by drug dealers. So this one Christmastime, the people who didn't care for that commerce went caroling at the drug dealers' homes. In the land of crack cocaine, "Frosty the Snowman" and "White Christmas" take on new meaning.

Troy will tell you their voices were bad enough to make dogs howl, but "we're just doing anything to agitate the drug dealers—in a good way, though."

It's not an easy task to confront your neighbors about their vices. It's not appreciated. One homeowner I met as I walked with the carolers told me that a lot of the singers made false accusations about him.

Caroled without cause?

"I'm tired of being harassed," he told me. Poor guy. Seems the drugs the police found weren't his—or have you heard this one? When I got back to the office, I checked the county Web site and found he was also a tax deadbeat. So I didn't feel too sorry for him. That was 2001. A few years later, he was charged with murdering a woman in Troy Hill. The message of the carols evidently did not take. The villain should have listened. He's in prison now, and can get his Christmas cards there.

Robin Troy is unflagging in her resolve to move her neighborhood in a better direction. She became exasperated one winter by people in the eight-unit building across the street routinely leaving garbage at the curb days before the pickup date. That trash would blow up and down the street, and her sixty-seven-year-old mother had to clean it up.

So one December—there's something about Christmas that brings out the festiveness in Troy—she gift-wrapped the garbage she collected in the street and mailed it to the Cranberry family that owned the building that spawned it.

If you live in the suburbs, that might shock you, but if you live in the city, you probably cheer that move. So many neighborhoods are plagued by absentee landlords who don't take care for their property, or rent blithely to problem tenants. While I sympathized with the suburban family that opened that foul, dripping package, I understood why a woman trying to carve a decent home for her children would suddenly go commando Santa.

So did Judge John Brydon of Butler County Common Pleas Court, who openly sympathized with Troy when she appealed her initial conviction for disorderly conduct. Brydon ultimately decided Ms. Troy had crossed a line but, perhaps inspired by Troy's use of "Santa" as the return address, Brydon employed logic reminiscent of the judge in *Miracle on 34th Street*. He said using the U.S. Postal Service made this a public act—one of the conditions for disorderly conduct—even if the destination was a private home. Then he fined her twenty-five bucks, less than a tenth of what he might have.

The yard across from the Troys remained a trashy mess when I checked it out around the time of her court hearing, but the street itself was clean as a whistle, likely because of the daily cleanups by Troy's mother, Ruth Thomas. The Troys' fenced yard was an oasis of green in an otherwise barren landscape, with a well-kept lawn, a swing set, picnic table and brick walkway. Troy admits it was rude to mail the garbage, but she can't shake her old-fashioned notion that when you buy a property, you are responsible for it. That much she'll never lose. People like her have kept and are keeping Pittsburgh going even as seemingly every cultural force is set against them.

It's just different in the city. Sometimes the rules need bent, as only a Pittsburgher would put it. Another woman in Troy Hill told me her trick regarding abandoned cars. The city won't come right away for vehicles ditched at the curb or in a vacant lot, but that city wind can blow awfully hard, sometimes so hard the car winds up in the middle of the street blocking everything. Then the city comes and tows it away.

Get it, boys and girls?

My neighbor Mark Fatla once called the owner of the office building next door to him because a private hauler was loudly picking up trash in the middle of the night, and told him, "I'm awake and now you are, too."

My neighbors won't abide outsiders making our lives less pleasant, be they Steelers fans blithely peeing their way through an autumn Sunday or absentee landlords having their garbage picked up in the wee hours of the morning. That office building with the nocturnal trash men has been sold since, and has been converted to six condominiums with second-floor patios starting at $300,000. Thus does a struggling city hang on. If this city is to be only an office park and place to watch ball games, it's doomed.

My neighborhood has rebounded to the point where some are making a monthly mortgage payment not much less than what it would have taken to buy the house in 1970. But I worry about other neighborhoods, not just those in the city but in the old streetcar suburbs surrounding us, all the places of the precious walkable life. The drug dealers have driven some away.

"Hunky Soul Food"

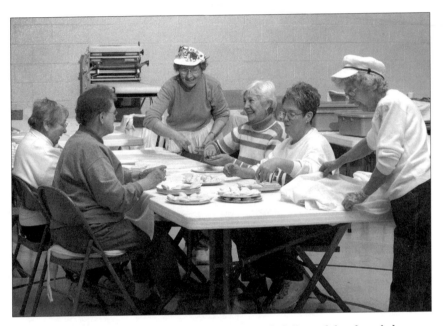

Churches and communities are held together with dollops of dough and cheese. Photo by Larry Rippel.

The women of Holy Ghost Byzantine Catholic Church in McKees Rocks have gathered every Friday morning, summers excluded, for better than fifty years. They come. They sit. They chat. They laugh. They put dollops of potato into little envelopes of dough.

It's nothing, really. And it's everything. By now, the church has third-generation pierogi pinchers.

But those born during the Baby Boom or later are the exception. Nearly all the women who shape the pierogis were born before World War II. Most are Carpatho-Rusyn, like Andy Warhol. They trace their ancestry to an area that covers parts of modern Slovakia, Poland, Romania and Ukraine. The recipe for stuffed cabbage you learned as a child largely depended on which valley of the Carpathian Mountains your parents were from.

It's like this in many an ethnic church in and around Pittsburgh. Daughters of miners and steelworkers, these women have seen their children scatter to suburbia. In our era of two-income families, there is little time for the old ways. But in the wee hours of the morning, women in their 70s and 80s will find their way into church kitchens they know as well as their own to sauté onions and make dough.

Helen Hopey, 84 and well into a 13-hour day on a Lenten Friday morning in 2008, was supervising the kitchen as Jayne Skreptach, 81, Ann Lubas, 83, Elsie Eberle, 80, and Peg Krulac, at 72 the acknowledged "baby" of the group, sat at tables pinching dough around dollops of cheese. Sauerkraut's the hardest pieorogi to assemble and potato the easiest, so the cheese is of middling difficulty.

As I tried my hand at the task, Mrs. Eberle shared stories of growing up there in The Bottoms, the part of McKees Rocks closest to the Ohio River. Her grandmother liked to tell of the night Elsie's mother Mary was born in 1903. Mary's father was across the river in old Allegheny City drinking heartily. There was no McKees Rocks Bridge then, and when he took the ferry back across, he slipped into the river. Or, as her grandma would tell it, "They were fishing him out of the Ohio while they were fishing Mary out of me."

When she was 8, Mrs. Eberle herself had to be lowered into a boat from a second-floor window during the 1936 St. Patrick's Day flood. She's been afraid of the water since, but when stories like that are told now, they're told for laughs or to pull like memories from friends.

The parents and grandparents of these women built this church with their nickels and dimes, so their children could be married there, and their children could be baptized there, and so on. How do they keep that chain from breaking? They gently press dollops of potato evenly down on small circles of dough and then bring the sides up to form an envelope, pinching carefully all around, and then repeat until another Friday morning is history.

The Reverend Ron Larko flips circles of dough down the tables faster than a Vegas blackjack dealer. He knew this was part of the job when he came to Holy Ghost from a church in Irving, Texas.

"This is the hunky soul food," a woman down the table interjected when the jokes began about jalapenos and taco sauce on Texan pierogis.

Such people keep us from becoming only a nation of subdivisions punctuated by chain stores. What happens when this generation goes?

Bob Tafelski, 49, has been coming over from Neville Island the past couple of years to volunteer in the kitchen. His wife takes Helen Hopey's water walking class just down the other side of the Ohio at the Sewickley Valley YMCA, and Mrs. Tafelski knew the pierogi detail could use another hand. "Why don't you come and help Helen?" she asked her husband, and Bob has been pretty much the Lone Baby Boomer since.

Will the next generation be there to carry the torch or, in this case, the sauerkraut? Often, when neighborhood traditions like this go, they stay gone. In March 2006, Anthony "Tony Chocco" Ciocca died, and his decades-long tradition of providing homemade Italian ices, made from fruit so fresh the seeds were still in the ice, died with him. The children of Morningside and Highland Park no longer have Tony's taste of summer. Those that did will never forget it.

The Holy Ghost Pirohi Project (our cantankerous town can't even agree on the spelling of its signature dish) may carry on forever. Some at the church think so. Others aren't sure, the world having changed so much since the first pierogis were carried out the door in the late 1940s.

The church is only a few miles down and across the Ohio from our house, but rarely have I remembered to drive there on Friday mornings, or to swing across the street for the haluski that came from heaven by way of the St. John the Baptist Ukranian Catholic Church. (Fridays were once more competitive than Sundays on Olivia Street, but I hear St. John's no longer has the people for haluski.)

Mostly I don't go. I forget, don't have time, don't make time, or don't bother, though I'll know I wish I did if the pierogi line disappears.

I once took a connoisseur of American folk fare to McKees Rocks for the holy starch fest. I'd met Randy Garbin, then of Worcester, Massachusetts, in a now defunct Downtown bar called The Chart Room in February 2001. A group called Ground Zero was meeting there every Thursday. This disorganization had the slogan "Revitalizing Downtown one beer at a time," and never troubled itself overmuch that its strategy hadn't made much difference. The dignity is in the struggle.

Into this group strode Garbin with a box of his magazines, *Roadside*. The magazine celebrated true Americana, the kind that still breathes and is not kept behind velvet ropes in museums or house tours. Garbin had just written his cover story "'Burgh Well Done!" and was ebullient, walking into a like-minded crowd. In an earlier incarnation, the bar had been a place where burlesque queens loafed, and it remained to its end a room where someone named Bubbles or Blaze could be comfortable, and what finer compliment could a saloon be paid?

"As I explored the city," Garbin wrote in *Roadside*, "I found myself baffled that anyone would complain about the entertainment options. I've since attributed such griping to youthful restlessness, because between Downtown, the South Side, the Strip District and Shadyside—not to mention all the other pubs, galleries, and theaters found tucked into all the little nooks and crannies of this town—one could spend a lifetime and not get to everything."

By then, Garbin had already explored Wholey's Fish Market in the Strip and The Oyster House in Market Square. They fit nicely with his recipe for an American renaissance, perhaps the best primer on the good life that can fit on a business card:

"Eat in diners. Ride trains. Shop on Main Street. Put a porch on your house. Live in a walkable community."

So I gave him directions to my house and the next morning he showed up and we rode to McKees Rocks to eat heavy. With a job that allowed Garbin to live anywhere, he even began searching Pittsburgh for a house with a porch. He swore he didn't tell that to all the cities, and he never did find the right situation for himself here, but he did find Mother of Sorrows Roman Catholic Church in Stowe to be the place to buy pizza, sausage rolls and spinach roll. He wound up his weekend by giving directions to the starch fest on National Public Radio.

In a very short time, Garbin did something I've seen often from out-of-towners. He embraced parts of the city that many native Western Pennsylvanians never see, or are too afraid or indifferent even to find out about. Garbin had that tremendous feeling of being in on a secret, one that those who shuttle only between the Olive Garden and Applebee's will never know.

I often joke that white flight has been very good to my family. We'd never have been able to afford a house like ours if "inner city" had not become a pejorative term. Local TV stations often cover the North Side the way the networks cover Baghdad, and that also keeps city real estate affordable. Sometimes I feel like shouting to the natives something akin to that traditional baseball heckle, "Hey, ump, you're missing a great game!"

People, you're missing a great city!

The Geography of Friendship

Beech Avenue on the North Side. Photo by Larry Rippel.

In 1992, *The Pittsburgh Press* took its own life after losing a public relations war with the Teamsters. Number crunchers in Cincinnati, home of the Scripps-Howard chain, wanted the company's largest newspaper off the books before New Year's Day. So it sold *The Press* to a newspaper that would kill it, my new employer, the *Post-Gazette*. Many good journalists and friends weren't so lucky and had to leave town.

Yet that was still a good year for me because, during that strike, I met the woman who would become my wife, Betsy Blazek. A child of Wisconsin's Northwoods, Betsy had come to Pittsburgh in 1991 for her first job as a physician. Her specialty is physical rehabilitation, and I remain a work in progress.

Betsy had moved here partly because Pittsburgh reminded her of Milwaukee, where she'd gone to medical school. When I met her, she was living in the East End because it was almost Pittsburgh law at the time that newly arriving singles make camp in leafy, trendy Shadyside for at least their first year.

I'd followed that rule, but by the time I met Betsy, I had moved from a Shadyside apartment to the North Side rowhouse. She was living just a couple of blocks from my old building on Highland Avenue, but her take on Pittsburgh was decidedly different. For starters, Betsy was forever riding her bicycle to Squirrel Hill for groceries and such, while my bike remained in dry dock. She was also big on taking in the countryside. She took me on hikes—hikes, for the love of trail mix—to Bear Run, Beechwood Farms, Raccoon State Park and points beyond. She taught me to cross-country ski well enough that I've skied to work after a couple of blizzards, and she got me back into a canoe for the first time since I stopped caring about merit badges. She had me traveling the same way Meriwether Lewis did when he floated a locally made keelboat down the Ohio in the summer of 1803 to explore the West. Betsy opened Pennsylvania to me.

Sometimes, in the dismal days of winter, it's easy to forget we live in a beautiful part of the world. Pennsylvania claims the most rivers and streams of any state in the lower forty-eight, yet until I met Betsy, I'd been missing all but the biggest. I'd spent nearly my entire adult life in and around the Appalachian Mountains, from Syracuse, where I went to college, to southwest Virginia, where I worked for almost a decade, but I'd pretty much blown off the natural landscape for the comforts of asphalt and concrete. My idea of roughing it was mixing my own drink. It took a Midwesterner to show me Penn's Woods.

I've since carried Betsy's ethos back to our city, learning to look closer at a place that is, mile for mile, about as green as an eastern American city gets (and as gray as any can get each winter). We have more acres of park per capita than any city in America. Throw in thirty-six miles of riverfront, and we're spanned by more bridges than any place this side of Venice. But those are just stats from the last Pittsburgh propaganda video I watched. I'm not even sure I buy that parks boast, but I do believe you need to get out there and see this place for yourself.

I remember a winter night, more than a half-dozen years ago, when balloons flew across the street at the McCarthys' house. At least I see balloons now; whether they were still there that night, I can't say. But I am sure that either the third or fourth McCarthy child had been born, William or Mary, because I had walked out to my stoop alone to smoke a cigar that John McCarthy had handed me days before.

I'm not a big cigar guy, but it felt right that night. It was a cold, clear evening, and the stogie went well with the dusty bottle of cognac I'd pulled from the back of the liquor cabinet. I smoked joyously and sipped from a snifter, trying to feel as much like Thurston Howell III as possible.

Taking in my street, I decided I didn't like it. I loved it.

Beech Avenue is canopied its two-block length with trees, none of them beeches, and flanked with faux (leave it to the French to make "fake" sound classy) Victorian street lamps. Everything on our street looks pretty much as it did in 1890, apart from the carriages, which are all horseless now. Not being far from decidedly bleak territory, it can take newcomers by surprise.

Let John McIntire, the talk show host, blogger, and stand-up comic, tell it. On Steelers Sundays, McIntire would park his car in the alley behind a long-abandoned A&P that stood, aching, about a half-block down and an alley up from our house.

"Too cheap to park to go to a game," McIntire says, "I park behind an abandoned warehouse wondering about the wisdom of leaving my car in a questionable area, step over a couple of drunken crackheads, walk a few feet, turn the corner out of the alley, and suddenly it's like a Disney movie. The sun is shining, the birds are singing, a little curly-headed blond girl rides her bike down the street. *Brrrrrrrring Brrrrrrrring* goes her bicycle bell. Squirrels scurry up and down the majestic old oak trees. Geese fly overhead. Kitty cats dart in and out of their well-kept yards. People actually smile at you, even if you don't belong there. The residences are all majestic old buildings oozing with character. For two long blocks or so, it's an absolute utopian urban paradise.

"Then you turn left toward the stadium and are confronted by dozens of drunken Stiller fans, along with some angry lottery losers ripping up their tickets and creating more litter outside the 7-Eleven, and the fleeting utopia seemed only but a dream."

OK, McIntire exaggerates. The trees aren't all oak, most kids aren't blond and that warehouse was actually once a supermarket. It was vacant for nearly four decades, far longer than it had been open, before it was leveled in the fall of 2006 to neighborhood cheers, making way for high-end homes (someday, we hope). Moreover, most of the crackheads I've met are ambulatory. Not that I've met many. What most people see of life on the North Side from local television news is about as close to our daily experience as mistletoe is to guided missiles.

But on that short stroll, McIntire can see almost everything to love and hate about life in our city. Our street surprises newcomers because such streets are no longer supposed to exist. They're not part of The Plan, the only federal program almost everyone still swears by.

The Plan is easily explained. In the early 1950s, President Eisenhower thought it prudent to make it possible for Americans to skedaddle from cities in one big heart-thumping hurry. Ike was only a handful of years removed from a little thing called World War II, where he learned to appreciate those sleek German autobahns that allowed enemy trucks to advance or retreat quickly. With a Cold War on, Ike figured America could use all the superhighways it could pave. And we started remaking our cities to suit them.

"Our roads ought to be avenues of escape for persons living in big cities threatened by aerial attack or natural disaster," Ike said.

Scatter buildings and people. Get commerce moving. Become harder for Soviets to hit. Americans, already in love with cars, didn't need much urging to suburbanize, but they got it anyway with the National System of Interstate and Defense Highways. That perfectly complemented federal loan policies launched in the 1930s that favored new homes over home repair (and quietly but explicitly promoted segregation).[3] Americans took to Ike's interstates like skaters to ice. Pittsburgh was no different. The planners of the 1950s would be scandalized by my route home from work. I stride from the newspaper building through Point State Park, the one part of my trip where I must credit Ike-era planners; damned few slices of urban America can equal the view around the Point. But on the wide walkway of the Fort Duquesne Bridge—added to the bridge only in the 1990s, nearly three decades after it opened to cars—I continue past the scowls of motorists stuck in the nightly backup. I then stride betwixt the stadia and on up the hill through Allegheny Commons, the oldest park west of the Allegheny Mountains, to my 1870s-era home.

To a planner of the Eisenhower Era, almost everything about that trip is wrong. These big thinkers had visions for the lower North Side, none of which included a guy walking home like a refugee from a Norman Rockwell painting.

And here let me dwell a little on my own neighborhood, as it is the one I know best, and because it stands in pretty well for the city as a whole, which so often has been the victim of thinking that is oblivious to Pittsburgh's strengths, following models that fit it the way a glove fits a foot.

"North Side Study," published by The Pittsburgh Regional Planning Commission in 1954 called for leveling every home in the neighborhood we now call the Mexican War Streets, just north of the big park. That was a time when "the mere age of a house was evidence against it," Walter Kidney and Arthur Ziegler wrote in their 1975 book, *Allegheny*. (That age bias still pops up. One of the most frequent arguments for leveling the Mellon Arena to make way for a new hockey palace was that the arena was the oldest in the National Hockey League, which evidently means the league should level whichever ice house is oldest whenever a new one goes up somewhere else.)

Blind worshippers of the next new thing demolished more than five hundred buildings on the North Side in the 1950s, including the Market House that had stood since 1863. They ripped out what they saw as the diseased heart of Allegheny's historic downtown, laid out in 1787, replacing it with what looks like a bunker on steroids: the doomed Allegheny Center Mall, which didn't last thirty years. I touched on that in an earlier chapter. Now let me give a little more detail.

The über-planners' brainstorm was to build residential superblocks filled with low-rise uniform housing. As the authors of *Allegheny* put it, "The bland, budget-conscious architecture of the 1950s was to replace everything. . . . The stone carving would be crushed for fill, the molded woodwork would go up in smoke. . . . Elevated roads were to slice the West Commons in half."

Thankfully, Ziegler, architectural historian James Van Trump and countless unsung heroes bucked the idea of traffic roaring twenty-five feet overhead and the War Streets eventually became a swank address. These folks who just said "Noooooooo!!!!!!!!!" also saved our neighborhood, Allegheny West, and Manchester, a largely black community that probably has the finest stock of Victorian homes in the city. Our drafty fixer-uppers have fetched ever larger dollars these past few years, even as the city's financial crisis dominated the local news. Residents of these old homes and of the more modern apartments in Allegheny Center, everyone from art and culinary school students to young families to retirees, appreciate the convenience of the quick ride or walk across the yellow triplet bridges—the Roberto Clemente, the Andy Warhol and the Rachel Carson—spanning the Allegheny River to Town.

It's possible that with expensive gasoline and a growing consciousness (okay, a semi-consciousness) that America should not be held hostage to foreign oil, the older, walkable way of life will come back, even seem patriotic, but that may take a very long time. My joke always has been that the North Side is like soccer. It's the sport of the future, and always will be. It's bound to get kicked around more yet.

Check out the 1937 photo of old Beaver Avenue on the next page. See the vibrant street of shops in Manchester, and compare it to the desolate, soulless service road it has become today, a mere abutment to Route 65. The big road takes commuters in from the northern suburbs to earn their bread and then hightail it home, just as the government planned a half-century ago. Manchester lost its commercial avenue, the lifeblood of any walkable community, and never has recovered fully.

These were hardly the only Pittsburgh or American neighborhoods tortured by "renewal" in the 1950s and 1960s. Between 1949 and 1973, the federal government bulldozed 2,500 neighborhoods in 993 cities, knocking a million Americans out of their homes.[4] In her book *Root Shock*, Dr. Mindy Thompson Fullilove estimated about 1,600 of the leveled places were black neighborhoods. Notable among them was Pittsburgh's Hill District.

Anyone who has seen an August Wilson play would not be surprised that Dr. Fullilove described the Hill as "pound for pound" the most culturally important black neighborhood in the United States. In its prewar heyday, it incubated a tremendous jazz scene, hosted the legendary Pittsburgh Crawfords of the Negro League, and produced a national black newspaper in *The Pittsburgh Courier*. But the Hill was cut off at its knees by an 80-block demolition in the late 1950s. In the lower Hill, where Italian, Lebanese, Greek and Jewish immigrants lived together with recently arrived blacks from the South, about 9,000 housing units were conveniently deemed substandard and blown away along with 400 businesses. "There

Beaver Avenue, looking north from Columbus Avenue, Manchester, 1937 (above) and today (below). Note the Duquesne Light building in the distant left of both photos, about all that survived the wrecking ball. Top photo courtesy of Pittsburgh City Photographer Society, University of Pittsburgh. Bottom photo by Larry Rippel.

would be no social loss if they were all destroyed," argued City Councilman George Evans in a 1943 article, brazenly outlining plans for a postwar Pittsburgh well before the war was over.[5] That grand plan spawned the Civic Arena, a highway ditch, a hotel and a high rise or two, but little else that's still around but the largest park-for-pay lot in Western Pennsylvania.

Even allowing for an overly nostalgic view of the past, the before and after photos of the Civic Arena site betray the hubris of civic destruction. Think of a place as an organism and it shouldn't be surprising that Pittsburgh fell on hard times after its leaders tore into its heart, eliminating old neighborhoods east and north of Downtown.

In 2008, Hill District residents rightly fought for a binding community benefits plan to go with the new arena. Reconnecting Downtown with what is, geographically if not literally, the residential heart of Pittsburgh will not only be crucial for the Hill, but for Pittsburgh.

My neighborhood, Allegheny West, was mostly spared such "progress," but residents have had to battle the Community College of Allegheny County and the Steelers to keep it a place to live rather than just a place for students and football fans to park. An auto-centric world is forever barking at our borders.

The Community College of Allegheny County tore down mansions on the south side of Ridge Avenue in favor of the aggressively functional buildings popular in the 1960s and 1970s. A walk down Ridge is now a study in architectural schizophrenia, with the southern side looking as if it were designed by Mr. Brady in his leisure suit and the northern side looking like the set of a Merchant Ivory costume drama.

Allegheny Avenue, our western border, is likewise a muddle. You've seen this commercial strip even if you haven't. It could be the encyclopedia illustration for Anywhere, USA, though it would face thousands of contenders: a defunct gas station, a Wendy's (where there used to be a Burger King), a McDonald's, a 7-Eleven and a Subway (that used to be a Rally's). It's the landscape of our frenzied culture, eye-catching yet dull, heavy on the plastic, low on the unique, all chained up.

Betsy and I are not zealots against modernity, mind you. Our daughters, Curran and Clare, born in 1998 and 1999, know the Krispy Kreme selection in the 7-Eleven as well as they do the children's section in the Carnegie Library. One winter Sunday afternoon, we were in that Wendy's. We just wanted to get the girls out of the house, so the four of us walked the block and a half for chocolate frosties.

As I sat there, waiting for the happy slurping to end, my eye was caught by the gothic steeple of Calvary Methodist Church—just beyond the sky-high, bright red McDonald's "Drive-Thru" sign. American history professors could hold classes in that Wendy's. Most of the story of the past century could be seen in panorama from our table. You could hit every fast food joint from the mountains to the prairies to the oceans white with foam and never see all this:

Starting with the window behind us and swiveling counterclockwise, south to north, I could see the castle-like PPG Place, creation of the architect Philip Johnson, across the river. Closer to us, on our shore, was Heinz Field, home of the Steelers and University of Pittsburgh Panthers. Up the hill on Ridge Avenue, a mansion, from the era when Allegheny City had the most millionaires per capita of any city in the world, had become a halfway house. Next door, another iron baron's mansion now owned by the community college, is haunted by the ghost of a maid scary enough to keep some college security guards from working alone at night. (It's true; I've asked.) Coming up a block to North Lincoln Avenue is the home of the Rooneys, owners of the Steelers and more rooted on the North Side than most of our trees (which I say with no small affection for that remarkable family). Next door is a former mansion now split into apartments, and a plaque announces it was the home of Harry K. Thaw, the man for whom the term "playboy" was coined. (On the roof of Madison Square Garden, Thaw blew the brains out of famous architect Stanford White, who cuckolded him, and then Thaw beat the murder rap with a plea of temporary insanity, making his lawyers the Johnnie Cochrans of the Ragtime era and making us oddly happy to think of Harry as a North Lincoln Avenue boy.) Then there's the McDonald's, which overtook a site once occupied by Laughlin mansions, as in the Jones & Laughlin Steel Company, making this a summary of American economic history from 1870 to 1970 in one parking lot. Finally there is the Calvary Methodist Church, where none other than Louis Comfort Tiffany himself provided the stained glass windows.

I could go on. Maybe I should. Most of the college kids riding in on the 16D or the 500 don't know half this stuff. When I moved to the neighborhood in 1990, I didn't either. I cared only about being able to walk to big-league ballgames, a boyhood dream. Then I settled in and discovered

Before and after in the Lower Hill District: The overlay for the Civic Arena and highways in what was once a densely populated neighborhood, and what it looked like after the buildings were blown away. Courtesy of the Pennsylvania Room of the Carnegie Library of Pittsburgh.

that when you live on a street where the buildings hug each other, you can't help but feel part of something bigger. You live among people who zigged when the world was telling them to zag. They move in mysterious ways.

In 1982, my neighbors decided they wanted brick sidewalks, and so they spent most of their spring and summer weekends laying bricks they'd bought by the tens of thousands for 6 cents apiece. The city had loosed this amateur mason's bonanza by razing an old slaughterhouse on Herrs Island, just a couple of miles up the Allegheny River, to make way for the high-end townhomes of "Washington's Landing," yet another instance of successfully cashing in on the future Father of Our Country's reckless adventures hereabouts.

By stroke of luck, the unloading of bricks coincided with the arrival of construction crews hired to install Victorian-style street lighting. For a few extra thousand, they agreed to haul away the concrete sidewalks, too.

"About this time," recalled John DeSantis, who led our neighborhood junta back then, "the police arrived and wanted to know why we didn't have sidewalks."

Two Beech Avenue men earned hernias schlepping curbstones, and the project that was supposed to end around Memorial Day ended around Labor Day, but the result is one of the finest nineteenth century streetscapes in America. Hollywood loves it, which is why some of the most egregious uses of film in cinematic history have been in our neighborhood.

That TV movie where Meredith Baxter plays a drunk and Christopher Reeve a child molester? That's one of ours. The flick with Don Rickles and the babe from *La Femme Nikita* working together to show us what it's like when vampires are in The Mob? That's ours, too.

Proud? Betcha.

On that second movie, *Innocent Blood*, my neighbor, Dave Teece, and I spent a good hour drinking beer on his second floor balcony, patiently waiting for a stunt vampire to make her jump from a Calvary Church gargoyle across the street. She finally did, too, falling at least as far as the director on the sidewalk below, John Landis, had since *Animal House*. You don't get to see that when you live on the end of a cul de sac.

My favorite neighborhood movie, though, was one I've never seen: *Darrow* starred Kevin Spacey and Chris Cooper before either one sniffed an Oscar. I've never run across it on video or DVD, but I know *Darrow* made our street look terrific because I was there when they filmed. The city Public Works Department covered the street with dirt and the movie people took down the street signs and painstakingly hid twentieth century electric meters, gas meters and fire hydrants with ivy, wooden fencing and barrels. Horse-drawn carts eased down the street. Neighborhood kids in Victorian costume were on the brick sidewalks playing baseball and skipping rope. A capped man riding a "penny-farthing" bicycle—with its large driving wheel in front and small training-sized wheel behind—glided along.

Just beyond the corner, cars continued up and down Allegheny Avenue, perpendicular to Beech; an overleaf of the past had dropped over a page of the present. The street was supposed to represent turn-of-the-century Chicago, but it looked as the city of Allegheny might have a century ago. I felt blessed to get a glimpse.

We go to strange lengths to preserve that nineteenth-century charm. One weekend every December, we get the cars off the street, and strangers pay good money to tour the houses. House tours are big across Greater Pittsburgh now, and we had one of the first about a quarter-century ago. The neighborhood council uses that money for everything from acquiring more property for renovation to throwing block parties to hiring hit ladybugs. We buy tens of thousands of those six-legged assassins every summer because, back in the 1970s, the city planted linden trees that are an aphid's dream. Those tiny, sluggish, sap-sucking creeps can drop goo on our cars thick enough to leave them as sticky as plates in a pancake house. You can't even roll down the windows—unless enough ladybugs arrive to chew through the aphids. For a while, we had a connection in Brooklyn who sold us serious eaters, but the first summer of the new century, the ladybugs we bought on McKnight Road exuded all the energy of your average doorstop. Sticky summer that.

Come to think of it, we're pretty big on fiddling with the ecological system. One Fourth of July, my neighbors flew two hundred pounds of live crawfish up from Louisiana, ate eighty pounds worth, gave forty to another party, and liberated the rest in the Allegheny River. Then they lost touch.

So why am I telling you all this? Because of a question that is so often in a stranger's eyes when I tell them my family lives in the city, most particularly the North Side:

Why in God's holy name would anyone want to live there?

If I'm in a hurry I answer by saying our family gets by with one station wagon that averages about seven thousand miles a year, including vacation trips. In an age of expensive gas, this alone wins converts. Not that seven thousand miles should sound paltry, as it could get you to California and back by way of Florida, but it might be one-fourth of what a suburban two-vehicle family logs in a year.

As a cheap, lazy man, that suits me. It also means less pollution and less oil imported from those people on the other side of the world who want to kill us. Plus all our walks generally give us the requisite hour of moderate daily exercise to keep the lard off. But truth be told, it isn't exercise, thrift, environmentalism or patriotism that keeps us where we are. The best way to explain what holds us, if I haven't already, is the parable of the garage door opener.

My neighbor, Tom Barbush, who has lived on the street since 1976, told me this story. A salesman for an East End printing firm, Tom is an old-school guy who quotes the Rat Pack the way some quote Scripture. He was sitting at lunch with a client who'd been through a recent divorce and was complaining about how tough it was to meet anyone. Trouble was the man's woes kept getting interrupted by people walking up to Tom to say hello.

So the guy asked Tom how he knew so many people. Tom asked if the man owned a garage door opener. When he said he did, Tom told him that was his problem.

"He looked at me like I was insane," Tom recalled. "But think about it. You hit the garage door opener. The door goes up. Car goes in. You're in for the night. How are you going to meet anyone?"

Tom parks his car at the curb. On a good evening, he may be locked out of the house, and his wife, Fran, has to figure out whose porch he wound up on. Or he takes in someone like me.

One glorious May evening, I walked home late from work and found myself without a key and nobody home. Betsy had taken the girls to the video store to bring back supplies to further distort their thinking, so I left a note in the door and walked down to the Barbushes. Tom pulled up as I arrived.

"I'm locked out," I told him.

"Let's have a beer," he said, adding as we walked through the side gate to his back porch, "I've been locked out of my house three or four times. It never failed to be a good thing."

He brought out a radio and this little tour of Pennsylvania he gives: Rolling Rock, Straub's, Yuengling, Iron City and Stoney's, though only the first three brands were cold. When we tuned in the Pirates game we found they had uncharacteristically scored a handful of runs early, and they increased their lead as we listened. Soon enough, Tom's wife, Fran, joined us, along with daughter Kate, home for the summer from Lehigh University.

Along about the fifth inning and my second Rolling Rock, the back door opened and my smiling Curran, then 4, came walking out to announce that they'd rented *E. T.* My wife followed with Clare, then two, with Betsy apologizing profusely for doing this very good thing to me, and Clare smiling at the possibilities of fresh territory.

Invited to stay, we did. Clare stacked rocks and looked for doodlebugs. Curran shadowed Kate and her sister, Liz, who'd just graduated from Oakland Catholic. Pretzels and chips were brought out, and so Liz walked over to our yard to retrieve some chives from Betsy's herb garden, which she diced into a dip.

The conversation wasn't important, though it ranged from the multimillion dollar plans for North Shore development (we gave that good reviews) to Kate's plans to visit her boyfriend in New York. (Those reviews weren't nearly so good, but later had to be revised; about five years later Kate married Brian Janes in St. Paul's Cathedral and our daughters were the flower girls. The Janeses now live in a riverfront apartment Downtown.)

We walked home later that evening. I ate a little cold chicken, listened to the last inning of the Pirates' win, then went upstairs where the four of us got in one bed and I read *If I Ran the Circus* by Dr. Seuss. Soon enough we were all asleep.

It was close as anyone is likely to get to a perfect night. If this world is short of anything, it is of legitimate excuses for adults to walk down the street to see if anyone wants to come out and play. I vowed that night to forget my key at least three more times before Labor Day, though, of course, it didn't work out that way. You can't plan serendipity. But you can plan communities so that casual meetings are commonplace, and those aren't the kind of communities America has been building for the past sixty years. Pittsburgh still has them everywhere.

The Barbushes aren't supposed to be where they are; America didn't plan for them to buy on our street. America tried very hard, in fact, to talk them out of it. Few were the believers in our neighborhood in the Bicentennial Year. Most of the large homes had long since become rooming houses. Some would say flophouses. But when the Barbushes saw they could buy a 3,000 square foot rowhouse on our street for $8,250, they bit.

What did they know? They both grew up in Masontown, about forty miles south. They didn't realize that no bank would offer a mortgage on Beech Avenue or anywhere else in the so-called inner city.

"It couldn't be financed, couldn't be mortgaged," Tom remembered. "It was about to have the utilities turned off. It had no heat. It needed everything. When I tried to buy it, [the bank] wanted all these things fixed before I could mortgage it. They wanted me to do $20,000 worth of work before they would loan me $8,250."

When he pointed out the absurdity to the bankers, they gave him that "get the message" look.

Tom had a thousand dollars, so he went to the city Urban Redevelopment Authority to borrow money at 3 percent for heat and plumbing. His real estate agent ultimately sold him a $35,000 mortgage and he used that money for plastering and other work. The Barbushes had beaten the red liners.

They moved across town from their apartment in Regent Square and became the fourth owners of a century-old house. At that time, other young visionaries were doing the same thing on Beech and other North Side streets. Nobody had coined the term "yuppie" back then. These people were just trying the place out, buying what they could afford without any grand plan.

"It was 'make some money, fix the toilet,'" Fran Barbush said. "If the ceiling didn't fall in, it didn't get fixed."

"We were all young enough not to care," Tom said. "If it didn't work, oh well, I had the rest of my life to straighten it out."

By the time I bought my rowhouse on Lincoln in 1990, the neighborhood had been pretty much resettled by this new wave, but I could still get a mortgage a full percentage point below the market rate. Some years before, the city had begun pressuring the banks to make home loans in Pittsburgh or lose city business. All parties since have done well by that carrot-and-stick approach. The value of homes has soared. By 1994, when Betsy and I married, nearly every home in the neighborhood had been restored. So I sold at a nice profit and moved to Betsy's rowhouse on Buena

Vista (pronounced BYOON-uh VIST-uh; there are few pretensions in Pittsburgh). That's in the Mexican War Streets, a few blocks northeast.

Three years later, Betsy said she wanted a house with a yard. I told her we had a yard. We kept it down the street in West Park and the city mowed it for us. She didn't buy that so, in 1997, we bought a house with a side yard on Beech.

Why were we persuaded to undergo the colossal pain in the nether regions that constitutes a move of even a few blocks? Because turning on Beech one evening before our final decision, we found about five kids from three families playing "Red Light, Green Light" in the middle of the street. The game wasn't organized by adults. Kids were just playing. Moments like that make a neighborhood in an America that seems to be running out of them.

It is here that I must mention the "Wait'll you're" echo. Almost anyone buying a home in the city will soon encounter one. You'll hear it often if you express any satisfaction with your choice.

"You like the city? Wait'll you're older," suburban friends say knowingly. Then it's "Wait'll you're married." Then "Wait'll you're a parent." Finally comes the big one: "Wait'll your kids are in school."

I've passed through each stage and am still happy. We've had a few scrapes. On a walk to work through the park about a decade ago, I was jumped by three teenaged boys. To put it in the kindest way possible, their youth group was soliciting funds. When I indicated those funds would not be forthcoming, their pitch became more aggressive and, as Woody Allen might say, I had to slam my face into a fist and my back into a foot. But I held on to my money, and what commuter never had a fender bender?

Another time, a cop came to our door to tell us they'd just caught a young girl who had written something obscene on the hood of our white station wagon: "F—— yall." Naturally, we were offended. The O'Neills have gone through considerable trouble lugging our apostrophe around for the past 1,000 years, and here was this girl cavalierly dropping it from "y'all." I let her know we weren't happy about that before we went to court, and she agreed to work on her grammar. That said, we did find almost every other driver giving us the Pittsburgh left at the traffic lights before we got the "F—— yall" removed.

Those are no more reasons to move than a dangerous intersection in suburbia would be, but schools are a serious issue. They are the biggest reason city taxes are high, representing two-thirds of the 3 percent wage and half the property taxes. More to the point, the schools haven't been good enough to suit many families. Mark Roosevelt, great-grandson of that rough-riding president Teddy, began challenging any acceptance of mediocrity when he became schools superintendent in 2005, but the student population was in free fall. Between 2000 and 2008, enrollment dropped from thirty-nine thousand to less than twenty-seven thousand as the middle class headed for the suburban hills. The percentage of low-income students shot from 48 percent to 66 percent.[6]

Because school enrollment is more than 60 percent black, the knee-jerk reaction is to suggest "white flight" is entirely about race, which is wrong. Deciding where your children will spend their youth is far more complicated. Many middle-class black families have opted out, too. Economic class, that subject that Americans are even less comfortable facing than race, has just as much to do with where people decide to educate their children. A two-parent, middle- to upper-middle class family generally hangs with economic peers, and many city classrooms are short on them. Good schools generally have a lot of them. This region is blessed with a number of good schools, public and private, which means a strong competitor may be over the next hill. When people move, they're moving to something, and we're nothing if not a mobile society.

That said, my family benefited because the public school we chose, Allegheny Traditional Academy (ATA), was off most white people's radar when Curran started in 2003. And here was the manifest irony of the way the city achieved racial balance in so many classrooms: You were never more aware of your race than when you tried to get your kid into a school designed to teach them that race shouldn't matter.

Allegheny Traditional is one of about thirty magnets in the city. Each school has a specialty such as a foreign language or the performing arts. The program began in 1979 as a way to achieve racial balance voluntarily. Our school, ATA, mandates uniforms, stresses citizenship and has wonderful music and arts programs. Half the spaces in each classroom were reserved for African-American students, the other half for everyone else. If you're old enough to remember the 1970s TV show *Room 222*, that's pretty much how the student body of the school looks, only the kids are smaller, in uniform and much less hairy.

We chose ATA after scouting other schools. We didn't like our neighborhood public school, which was farther away than the magnet, anyway. We liked Incarnation Academy, a dynamic little Catholic school on Observatory Hill that since has closed, but we couldn't walk there. We also liked Phillips Elementary, a magnet school on the South Side that offers Spanish, but going there would have meant having our five-year-old on the corner around 7 a.m. Children need sleep. So we kept coming back to the closest school to our home, ATA, housed in a grand old brick building in the center of our park. It was once Allegheny High School and the novelist Willa Cather taught there in an earlier building.

Our firstborn was a lock to get into ATA because she is white and lives in the neighborhood. That sounds crass, but in the initial registration for the two kindergarten classes in 2003, thirty-five black children signed up for twenty-six slots, so nine had to go on a waiting list. Only nineteen "other" children signed up for the remaining twenty-six slots, so all of us "others" were accepted immediately.

It's more than a little odd to think that in Pittsburgh, the whitest large metropolitan area in the country, my pale family benefited from quotas, but it did. In another part of the city, a black family might have had a surer shot at a given magnet. You wouldn't think so much would still ride on pigment and geography a half-century after the U.S. Supreme Court declared that "segregated schools are not equal and can't be made equal," but that's the way it worked until recently. A narrow Supreme Court decision in 2007 striking down race-based enrollment criteria forced the Pittsburgh School Board to shake up the magnets. In April 2009, it dropped the 30-year practice of reserving up to half the seats in magnet classrooms for black students. Starting in the fall of 2010, a weighted admissions lottery, taking into account factors such as proximity to the school and eligibility for free or reduced-price lunches, will take effect.

I hope the magnets don't change much. The subtle nods to racial balance can be funny. When Curran was in kindergarten, my wife and I were part of an enthusiastic crowd that packed the auditorium to see the kids put on a Motown revue. You haven't heard "Stop! In the Name of Love" until you've heard five-year-old girls belt it out with little palms pushed defiantly at stumbling five-year-old boys. The next December, the same kids gave us a "Holiday Hoedown" with cowboy outfits and two kinds of music: country and western.

I believe that no musical education would be complete without both

Smokey Robinson and Hank Williams, and even the dullest among us has to see that All-American entertainment forms such as tap dancing, jazz and rock 'n' roll evolved only because descendants of Europeans and Africans traded moves, chords, and instruments in the home of the brave. But I don't think about that when I have our camcorder pointed at the ATA stage. I just want to keep our daughters in focus.

We won't lose that focus. Diversity isn't the reason our daughters are in school. Education is. The former can help with the latter, but the two also have been known to get in each other's way. We are thus far happy with our choice. As I write, our girls are in fourth and fifth grade, though our hopes of seeing ATA become a de facto neighborhood school, like Linden in the East End, have diminished as our economic peers have turned to private schools. We've been to a neighborhood meeting, called by parents of toddlers worried about test scores the way coal miners worry about keeled-over canaries. We tell them ATA has been very good for our girls. But like any conscientious parents, black or white, we'll take another option if that proves best.

Kindergarten students at the Allegheny Traditional Academy perform "Stop! In the Name of Love" *in 2000. Darrell Sapp*, Pittsburgh Post-Gazette.

One of the nice things about Pittsburgh is that world of choices, particularly if one has the means, which brings me to another little oddity about life in the inner city, or at least this city. Clare first went to kindergarten at Cardinal Wright, the Catholic School next door to ATA, because she was eight weeks too young for public school enrollment in 2004, and we didn't want to send her to another year of pre-school. (She'd been in one so long, we feared she'd be given tenure.) So for one year our girls, born nineteen months apart, went to different schools together, their campuses side by side.

Both schools were great, but when Clare moved up to first grade, we took advantage of the sibling preference and enrolled her in public school with her big sister. Though I'm an active member of St. Peter parish, which supports Cardinal Wright, we intend to make use of the city schools as long as they remain useful, particularly now that The Pittsburgh Promise is offering help with college tuition to city students. (More on that shortly.)

What's funny about the hoops we jumped through to get into ATA is that the year Clare was in kindergarten in Cardinal Wright, the racial makeup of her class was pretty much the same as Curran's. Integration came about in the best possible way, naturally, as parents made choices that suited them. So let me just take a moment here to hit my knees and thank God for the Catholic, Jewish and other religious schools in the city that keep neighborhoods strong by giving families reasons to stick around, at no expense to taxpayers beyond the buses some ride.

None of that means everything is hunky-dory in city education. The city gave Superintendent John Thompson his walking papers in 2005 because he'd evidently never picked up a Pittsburgh newspaper. I make that assumption because Thompson blithely proposed a 22 percent property tax increase in the midst of the city's fiscal crisis, showing he had no clue about one of the chief reasons the city teaches fewer children each year. The school board, to its credit, held the line on taxes and decided to look elsewhere for the next superintendent, ultimately hiring Roosevelt, who came in slashing.

Some charged racism because Thompson is black and Roosevelt is white, as were six of the nine school board members, but the color in play here is green. If we're going to pay someone $185,000 a year to oversee a $530 million budget, that person needs to recognize the competition over the hill. Thompson once told me that taxes in the city weren't high and it was a privilege to pay them. He was wrong twice.

Roosevelt's father was the Central Intelligence Agency operative who engineered the installation of the Shah of Iran in the 1950s, but overhauling the Pittsburgh schools may be more of a challenge. Lately, Roosevelt and the school board have made tough decisions, closing more than twenty schools to keep taxes where they are, and following that up the next year by trimming more than two hundred additional jobs. That process hasn't been pretty. Schenley High School, a good school with a diverse student body, was closed in 2008 because of an abestos problem, and that decision had some parents calling for Roosevelt's head. There also have been all too familiar slipups like having to pay highly paid assistant superintendents huge money just to go away, middle school students feeling cheated by winding up back in a K-through-8 setup, and parents wondering why schools seemed to be pinballing from K-8 to 6-12 setups. But our much maligned and unpaid city school board has made tougher choices than most of their suburban peers. Twenty suburban school districts in Allegheny County raised their real estate taxes in 2004 by at least one mill. (That's one dollar for every $1,000 in property valuation.) Ten districts raised taxes by at least two mills. Even before those whopping increases, the city schools had the lowest millage of any system in the county. That's deceiving out of context, given that city schools are also tapping working residents for a 2 percent wage tax, but holding the line on taxes shows fiscal resolve.

Anyway, on prettier mornings, Curran and Clare walk to the schoolhouse door, or they ride their bikes and lock them to a parking meter across the street. On uglier days, one of us drives them over. One winter morning, when Curran was in kindergarten, I even pulled her to school on a sled, sliding her across that tundra in a conscious effort to burn in good memories before she becomes a teenager and turns on me.

My wife is a physician and works part time so, most days, Betsy would meet the girls at the door when school let out, and the three of them dawdled home together. Now and again, I joined these family treks, with the leaf-pile jumps and snowball fights and squirrel feedings from the peanuts Betsy keeps in a coat pocket. But most of the time their homework is done by the time I get home. Both girls are thriving and Curran has been accepted in the city's middle school for the creative and performing arts, where we hope Clare will follow. In short, we have no reason not to stick with the schools of our city—particularly now that The Pittsburgh

Promise has arrived.

The Pittsburgh Promise might be the best thing to happen to the city in generations, bigger than any Super Bowl win—if it works. The Promise is that by 2012, every city resident who graduates from a public city high school with at least a 2.5 average will be eligible for up to $10,000 a year in scholarship money. That offer is good at any private or public college in the state, from trade schools to the University of Pennsylvania. The high school graduates of 2008 got up to $5,000 in the first year to kick off the program.

That could change the city-suburban dynamic dramatically. Instead of real estate agents telling every prospective homeowner to move to the suburbs to avoid the city's 3 percent wage tax, they can tell two-child families, hey, you could be looking at $80,000 toward your children's futures if you can find a good city school.

Of course, The Promise could fail. It needs a $250 million endowment to succeed. The University of Pittsburgh Medical Center (UPMC), the job-rich giant that dominates the region in much the way U.S. Steel did at mid-century, kicked in $10 million just before Christmas in 2007 and promised $90 million more on the condition that everyone else kick in $135 million. Then The Promise almost died before it was born in a flap over future tax credits. Never mind that non-profit hospitals don't even pay property or payroll taxes. This is Pittsburgh. We are more than willing to go to the mat over hypothetical questions.

Anyway, that was cleared up in a couple of weeks and now we will watch to see if The Promise can answer Pittsburgh's big question: How can a city survive when its largest employers, unlike the steel mills that preceded them, are mostly untaxed and workers' freedom from that wage tax is an easy commute away? Maybe you survive by giving people something they can't get anywhere else. You give them a safe, walkable, interesting city with decent schools and add an incentive so big it lights up the future.

UPMC wasn't playing Santa Claus. It was protecting itself. Almost eleven thousand of its employees live in the city and its future is bleak if the neighborhoods sink around it. Beyond that, Western Pennsylvania needs to incubate an educated workforce because it has had next to no luck attracting newcomers.

Many say UPMC, with $93 million in net income in the quarter before The Promise was unveiled, didn't give enough. People living in other communities where UPMC has a footprint wondered why it wasn't contributing to college dreams there. City residents with children in Catholic and other private high schools felt they should be covered by The Promise, too. Some UPMC employees wanted the money to go into their paychecks. Some patients wanted discounted care. Or more nurses. And so on. Maybe, one day, there will be money to extend The Promise, but as I write it's not at all clear The Promise can even meet its announced goals. If the most hopeful bet on the city in memory fails, Pittsburgh will keep sinking. Nobody has to look hard to see the signs.

Saving the Best

The now-closed Wilksboro Avenue bridge, a ninety-foot tall, one hundred year-old steel footbridge in the Brighton Heights section of the North Side. Lake Fong, Pittsburgh Post-Gazette.

It's a measure of Pittsburgh's mystery that I can still find wonders less than three miles from my neighborhood more than a decade after my arrival.

On city maps, Wilksboro Avenue looks like a mundane east-west connector in the Brighton Heights section of the North Side. But if you want to get from Termon Avenue to California Avenue that way, you have to get out of your car, because the full length of Wilksboro includes a nineteenth-century steel footbridge that is three hundred seventy feet long and eighty-six feet above the ravine below.

Before his job was eliminated in the cost-savings purge of 2004, City Engineer Fred Reginella advised against taking this route, saying the bridge is in serious disrepair. With fifty-eight tons of steel, it cost only $3,060 to build in the 1890s, but the city couldn't possibly spare the $70,000 it would cost to demolish it. It might be too fragile even to sandblast and re-paint, not that the city can afford the quarter million dollars that would be required. In the summer of 2007, the city finally fenced it off and it hardly seems likely a strapped city will find the funds to repair this wonderful antique soon. In 2009, the city spent $750,000 to implode the decaying Davis Avenue Bridge in Brighton Heights, and its replacement is years away.

So it remains, high and hidden in a part of the city that looks like the country, and those of us lucky enough to have used it, even if it was only a few times, feel its loss. On the June morning that Betsy and I crossed it together for the first time, an orange and black blur flew past, above the treetops, yet at our eye level. It was the first time I could remember seeing a Northern Oriole anywhere other than on a baseball cap.

There was no sense of danger when we walked the bridge, no need for Indiana Jones bravado, no Shrek-and-Donkey wobble in the knees. The rusting bridge, crossing a ravine, felt as sturdy as any sidewalk. Its peeling green paint was hardly noticed with robins and sparrows in full song and a squirrel high in a tree thirty feet below.

For Tiffany McCary and Damia Smith, teenagers we met that morning, it was also the key to their route to the bus stop on California and the Giant Eagle on Brighton Road. Without it, they would need to walk an extra mile around.

That same afternoon, I returned for another look and saw a second pair of teenagers crossing the bridge, with no more care than you might have crossing the room. You can bet such day-in-the-life trips will be ones they'll tell their grandchildren about.

I called the Audubon Society after seeing the bridge in 2004 because I had this fantasy of birdwatchers regularly flocking to the bridge, chasing any bad apples to more secluded spots. Maybe some rich birders could even fund the bridge's restoration.

Not going to happen, I know. But it's a shame that previous generations left Pittsburgh with all this cool stuff, and here we are, saving up just to blow treasures away.

Thanks, I'd Rather Walk

An after-school stop since "your dad was a lad": Clare O'Neill, Kiki and Mia Michelbacher, and Curran O'Neill get some ice balls and popcorn from Gus Kalaris, circa 2003.

You know those Christmas catalogs that show wintry Victorian streetscapes, dotted with smiling walkers carrying packages? That would be our life if we had anywhere in our neighborhood to shop. We envy those city and suburban neighborhoods with walkable commercial districts, such as Mt. Lebanon, Squirrel Hill, Lawrenceville, Bellevue, Bloomfield, Dormont and Oakmont. But we can walk to work, to school, to church, to the bank, to the YMCA and to the Children's Museum, a marvel with one building from each of the past three centuries.

In summer we walk to the park for the swings and slides and ice balls, which Gus Kalaris has been serving from his orange cart topped by a wide umbrella "since your dad was a lad." On weekends, we walked for years to Beleza, the coffee shop in the War Streets, where Clare developed a taste for bagels with cream cheese washed down with green apple soda, and Curran for a chocolate chip cookie and hot chocolate. Beleza's owners folded the tent in the spring of 2009, but by then Hoi Polloi had opened just around the corner from us, where I finished writing this book and our kids like the Nutella sandwiches almost as much as I like the eggs.

We used to walk to the first publicly funded Carnegie Library in the world, in little Andy Carnegie's old neighborhood no less, until one night in the spring of 2006 lightning lopped off the top of the clock tower, sending parts of it crashing through the building. (Clare and I were running from a school dance to our car during that thunderstorm and we heard the knee-rattling clap not one hundreds yards from us. The grand building has been repaired, but is no longer a library; its replacement is a more modern but less regal building on Federal Street. That's yet another sign of the times. This strapped city must trade grandeur for functionality at almost every turn. Still, I hope that someone reading this has checked it out from the new Allegheny branch.)

We walk to the National Aviary and the Carnegie Science Center and to Pirates games in North America's prettiest ballpark. We can walk to Giorgio's for pizza and cheese tortellini with sausage, or to the Allegheny Sandwich Shoppe where the neighborhood lays waste to Greek omelets. We go to Peppi's, whose owner grilled his way into regional fame by throwing together beef, sausage, scrambled eggs and cheese and calling it a "Roethlisburger" after the Steelers quarterback. We used to carry a bottle of wine to go with dinner at Muriel's, a fine Western Avenue restaurant that disappeared because not enough people found it. Now we do the same at Nicky's Thai Kitchen, its worthy successor. I sometimes go alone to The Monterey Pub for a shepherd's pie so rich the former owner, Joe Mansfield, used to claim "you can hear the arteries hardening clear to East Ohio Street." (Eating for the lower North Side cycle in less than ten days is not advised by the U.S. Surgeon General.)

We can walk to the Allegheny River shore and show our children where it meets the Monongahela to form the Ohio, as if they give a rip when we tell them the water flows clear to New Orleans. They part from us to

Let's get vertical! Betsy O'Neill competes in the annual Fineview Step-A-Thon 5K, climbing 381 of the 45,000 steps that are scattered throughout the city's 700+ public staircases. Annie O'Neill, Pittsburgh Post-Gazette.

play in the Watersteps, five hundred blocks of sandstone cut from a Butler County quarry that descend to shape a gentle, child-friendly waterfall that hugs the Allegheny's northern bank. (North Siders don't call it the North Shore; that's our south shore.)

A couple of generations ago, this kind of life would have warranted a "Yeah? So?" The walkable life was common for most Americans, whether they lived in small towns or big cities, but it is now decidedly retro. In 2007, the Brookings Institution said Pittsburgh was the ninth most walkable metropolis in the country.

Most of the rest of America has been driving in the other direction. My older sister, Anne, lives in a lovely modern suburb in Rhode Island called Coventry, and she tells the story of a teenaged neighbor, Teresa, getting permission to cross "The Big Road" to the shops on the other side. Crossing the state road is a rite of passage in her neighborhood, but the next year, my sister would see Teresa driving on that same stretch. People have to be hustled across the threshold from childhood to adulthood double-quick when the transitive steps are blocked by thirty-mile-an-hour traffic.

It doesn't work that way in old Pittsburgh. Take our park. Gus Kalaris serves peanuts, popcorn and snow cones—North Siders call 'em ice balls or icy balls or just "icies"—over by the tennis courts. Around here, Gus defines Pittsburgh summers. So much so that, back in 1998, when Gus had to stay home one kidney and one appendix lighter than he'd been at summer's start, it was like finding Kennywood amusement park closed.

"It's like a ghost town," Vince Parey, of Brighton Heights, said of the strangely cartless stretch of park. "Nobody on the benches. Nobody."

I visited Gus at home in Brighton Heights and he looked good, though much leaner. He joked that his epitaph would be, "I'd Rather Be at the Park," even as his wife and constant cartside companion, Stella, steered talk from premature talk of tombstones.

Stella urged baklava and other Greek pastries on me and Annie O'Neill, a former *PG* photographer who is no relation but a valued friend. Memories were poured with the coffee.

Stella, three years younger than Gus, born in 1932, met him when they were kids. She started helping at the cart when they were dating, and Gus hadn't missed a day since his father died in 1951. That means he hasn't seen a Pirates game since he went to see Jackie Robinson and the Brooklyn Dodgers play in Forbes Field in 1949, even though the games have been played just down the hill from him for close to four decades.

The Kalarises make it look easy, yet fourteen-hour days are Gus's norm. He spends three hours getting his wares together each morning, loading a Chevy van and the cart from the back of a Western Avenue building he owns, and then towing the cart behind his van to the park. Each day, he scrapes through several seventy-five-pound blocks of ice, one small paper cup at a time.

Parey, his neighbor, told me he tried scraping the ice once.

"I lasted ten minutes," he said. "My hand froze. My arm hurt."

"Rub a couple of twenties on it," Gus told him that day he was convalescing.

When I heard Gus say that, I knew he would be back, and he has been in all the summers since. But that year, even on the prettiest days, the park looked strange and unfamiliar, as if it were trying to smile with a tooth missing.

Another morning, another year, I was walking to work and found a couple of men high in the park's trees, brandishing fearsome blades that looked like they were lifted from the prop room of *Braveheart*. As one man swung from one sycamore branch to another with the aid of his safety rope, a sharp saw, shiny at the end of a ten-foot pole, dangled from his work belt. A shorter saw, pulled from a holster, helped him send a branch as thick as a ballplayer's bicep crashing to the ground.

I was transfixed, though also suddenly embarrassed by the meekness of my own tools: a cheap plastic pen and a notebook. I must have watched for a half-hour, watched as they nimbly moved up, down and across the branches of trees seventy-five feet high, watched as brush piles rose beneath them.

Sharp tools, a bird's eye view of the city and no boss in sight—what was not to like? So when the man in the Siberian elm climbed down, with the chill easing out of the morning, I asked about his work.

Larry Wolfe and his partner in climb, Dave Wharton, were then in their third winter pruning the Commons' eight hundred-tree variety pack. We're talking Norway, silver and sugar maples; American, fern leaf and European beeches; sweet gums, tulip poplars, cucumber magnolias, Kentucky coffee trees, crab apples, dawn redwoods, Douglas firs, bald cypresses, sycamores, London plane trees and six types of oaks. Some date back one hundred thirty years, and they'd been neglected for most of the past thirty, until the Garden Club of Allegheny County raised $180,000 in grants to return the trees to something of their former glory.

The club was led to this project by Christina Schmidlapp, who once lived on our street but moved to Oakland years ago with her husband, Ellis, and children Jane, Emily and Jacob. Hands-on philanthropy such as Christina's is the way it has to happen in Pittsburgh these days, with the city oh-so-beato, flat-on-its-seato broke. A neighborhood task force is busily seeking corporate and foundation funding for a park makeover.

In 2005, the city took a small stand for trees. City Council voted narrowly to use $109,000 from a federal Community Development Block Grant to buy a couple of hundred trees. It beat back a faction led by then Councilman, now Mayor, Luke Ravenstahl, which wanted more pavement, more street repair. His arch-rival, the East End Councilman Bill Peduto, won the argument for a greener choice. It was a mere gesture—the amount was about a third what a city our size generally spends on trees—but was nonetheless a strong one given the city's money straits, and was appreciated. The most desirable neighborhoods are the leafiest. Folks dig trees, and anyone who has ever walked in August from my shady street to the next block, barren and sizzling Western Avenue, can tell you there's no better way to assuage urban heat than with a line of trees.

Could walkable neighborhoods be more coveted in an age where we seek to stem our national addiction to imported oil? Where global warming is more than a theory? I think so, which would put Pittsburgh in good position for a comeback, because walkable neighborhoods became illegal almost everywhere else shortly after World War II. Modern suburban zoning, which leaves parks and commercial areas far from homes, makes the walkable errand all but impossible for most Americans because there is almost no place to walk to. And when people try to give their neighborhoods those human touches, beware. A code enforcement officer from the Too Much Fun Division may show up to shut things down.

I know this because, in the mid-1990s, Mike Ryan bunched up some bureaucrats' shorts in Bethel Park simply by putting up a basketball hoop on his front lawn, next to the curb. Ryan's Hoop became the hangout of choice on Opalwood Court for both kids and parents, and there were thirty-four children under the age of 11 on the cul-de-sac back then.

In an age when suburban parents too often have to drive their children to Activities with a Capital A, this backboard became an oasis of old-fashioned play. Its story could be a primer for countless American neighborhoods with similar recreational vacuums. Trouble for Ryan was the borough didn't plan it. So a government functionary ordered him to take it down, and had another fellow on a neighboring block do the same. The man on Stonewood Drive caved to the threat of a $500-a-day fine, but Ryan held his neighborhood's sacred ground. He found an ally in Councilwoman Susan Hughes, who said, "I'd rather hear the sounds of bouncing ball on a summer evening than have the kids with nothing to do."

Bethel Park's council twice directed its planning commission to come up with a more flexible ordinance and twice the commission said it couldn't. The alleged concern was safety, though it would be hard to imagine many places on Earth safer than the end of a cul-de-sac in Bethel Park.

Borough officials may have been chastened when this story hit my *Post-Gazette* column three years into the affair, because they soon told Ryan he could get a permit for the hoop, not that he bothered. He just left it up, and when that hoop finally gave out years later, it was succeeded by another, with the men of Opalwood chipping in for basketball equipment and beers, sending the former up as the latter went down.

In early 2006, there were still thirty-seven kids under the age of twenty on Opalwood, by the Ryans' count. The original kids had grown into musicians and champion swimmers. A new generation, and new families, still have a safe place within walking distance to pass the time, as do other families on the tree-lined streets of the South Hills town of thirty-four thousand now that Ryan's Hoop has paved the way for curbside play. Let's hope other suburban planners pay attention. Because too many have created a world where children have to get grownups to drive them everywhere, a world where there's no such thing as a corner store or barbershop for those countless casual encounters that can turn acquaintances into friends.

There is recognition of this around the country, and fans of the walkable life have made beachheads—or maybe I should say "beechheads"—but they are few. This movement is loosely labeled "The New Urbanism." Its most famous example is probably Celebration, the little boomtown Disney made from scratch in central Florida, with apartments above stores, a central commercial district and, well, pretty much all the basics found in Lawrenceville or Bloomfield or Squirrel Hill or Mt. Lebanon or Bellevue or Dormont or Wilkinsburg or Braddock or Zelienople, places either embraced or abandoned for reasons beyond their nineteenth-century design. I'm only half-joking when I say the shame about Pittsburgh is that we can pick only one neighborhood to live in.

Homage is also paid to new urbanism in twenty-first century shopping centers with neo-traditional streetscapes, such as SouthSide Works. Leaders in Cranberry are doing yeoman's work attempting to graft a walkable community to a sprawling 'burb, but it's difficult to take long, interesting walks when you're not working from the street grids common to pre-war communities. At more than one crossroad of Route 19, walking across the road is illegal in every direction at all times. Red-slash-through-the-pedestrian signs face all four ways. Reach any of these intersections without a vehicle and you have to go back home and get one. It's no wonder suburban kids are chauffeured everywhere. The modern suburb is designed for cars, not bipeds.

Developers know they can sell us nods to the past, but that's about as far as most go. The Waterfront, which opened on the Mon a dozen years after the sprawling Homestead Works steel mill shut down in 1987, has been hugely successful as a shopping and entertainment complex, but it essentially turns its back on the real town, the real deal, the real history, beside it in Homestead. The borough's old main street is dying on the vine as everyone goes right from the Homestead Grays Bridge to the new stores, theater and restaurants. Good luck to anyone walking from one of the new riverfront apartments in search of a quart of milk or box of cereal. Steelers backup quarterback Charlie Batch, a Homestead native, was awarded a half-million-dollar state grant in 2007 to convert an old bakery into sixteen loft apartments and a half-dozen commercial spaces, so we'll see if that's a start toward knitting together the new and the old.

The city's SouthSide Works, also built on the site of a razed steel mill, is a better visual fit with the surrounding neighborhood, but, like the Waterfront, its goal is to hold visitors until they're done spending. It still feels more like a movie studio's back lot than a real place. Few of those driving to the movies, bars, restaurants or shops there bother with any of the places farther down Carson Street. That said, the restaurants, coffee shops and Joseph-Beth Booksellers facing Carson make a connection, as do the dozens of new apartments just off the street. Perhaps this will be the development that segues into the old.

If grafting the new urbanism to the old is tough, think how much more difficult it is in a modern suburb. As the twentieth century was ending, a developer in the North Hills tried to re-create my nineteenth-century street near the booming crossroad of Routes 8 and 910. I drove up there in 1999 to reconnoiter "Beech Street at Richland," billed as being within walking distance of the Northtowne Shopping Center, the Richland Youth Center, the Gibsonia Post Office, a Giant Eagle, four banks, a gas station and "much, much more."

Leaving aside for a moment the absence of much reason to *walk* to a gas station beyond having a bottle of pop with Goober, the promotion of walking in the North Hills seemed a genuine throwback. So I drove out of the city on the Parkway North, a highway that demanded the extinction of the walkable East Street Valley neighborhood on the North Side. When I reached the site of Beech Street at Richland, I left my car and tried to walk to the places described in the promotion—and was nearly mashed in heavy twilight traffic on Route 8.

My mistake was taking the term "walking distance" literally. When I asked the developer if he really expected people to walk to Kmart like one of Richland's early settlers, he said no.

"They'll drive right across the street," Dr. Dominic Brandy said.

Old-time 'Burghers should recognize Dr. Brandy as the cosmetic surgeon and hair restoration guy from the television commercials, and he's a very nice fellow, too. Brandy explained to me that "walking distance" was a figure of speech in the North Hills, much like "stone's throw."

He wasn't kidding. I happened to be in the North Hills during a small evening snowstorm early in 2005, and drove through Beech Street at Richland. The quiet, prosperous development looked grand under its fresh white dusting. The architect had made flattering genuflections to my neighborhood, with wrought-iron railings, decorative half-moons at the rooftops and those wooden eyebrow thingies over the windows (as a child of suburbia, "eyebrow thingies" is the best I can do at describing Victorian architecture. To me, wainscoting still looks like someone ran out of paneling halfway up the wall.) These homes have sold in the past few years for $145,000 to $180,000 and look terrific. I'm sure they're filled with people as happy with their choices as we are. If I ever find myself dying to move to a place where I can't walk anywhere, Beech Street at Richland would make the short list.

Obviously, my biped leanings are not shared by most. A modern development needs no sidewalks, but must have off-street parking for at least two vehicles. These townhouses in Richland had roughly half the living area of homes on our street, but the finest among them had a two-car garage beneath. It's nearly impossible for a family in a postwar suburb to get by without two vehicles, hence the traffic jams on Route 910 that have prompted some neighbors to protest any new development. And, it should be added, many new townhouses on the North Side also have incorporated garages into their design, including the $300,000 condos at the end of my block in converted office space. Times do change, and even an inveterate walker such as I would never give up his driver's license.

The point here is not to get into a my-neighborhood-is-better-than-yours debate, though maybe I have slipped into one. What I value about

Beech Street in Richland Township (above) and Beech Avenue on Pittsburgh's North Side (below). Photos by Larry Rippel.

Pittsburgh and what suburban residents value about Pittsburgh don't have to be all the same things, because I'd bet the mortgage money that we have more in common than not. I'm less concerned with the new urbanism than I am with the old, maybe because I never have liked throwing things away. (You should see my T-shirt drawer.) It's painful to see a great city sink, even if Pittsburgh is one of many being tossed aside in our country. As Bernard-Henri Levy, a French philosopher who recently traced the footsteps of Alexis de Tocqueville through America, wrote in 2005:

> *I have seen so many unloved cities in America since this journey started. In my mind's eye there are so many cities half destroyed, or simply disfigured, by vandalism and the indifference of their inhabitants. Buffalo . . . Detroit . . . Cleveland . . . Lackawanna . . . . The cities die off, the great shattered cities of the American North . . . .*[7]

We can't let that continue in Pittsburgh, however far along the path to ruin we have wandered. We shouldn't get too hung up on counting people. A place can be prosperous without a growing population; my neighborhood is healthier today than decades back, when it was lined with rooming houses. On the other hand, it also seems clear that if the city continues to empty, the region is lucky to tread water. That's particularly crucial now that Pittsburgh is perhaps the most sprawling place on the American map.

That may sound nuts to anyone who has been to Atlanta or Los Angeles, but David Rusk, the former mayor of Albuquerque, has made the study of American cities his life's work, and Rusk says that in the last half of the twentieth century, the population of the Pittsburgh region grew by only 14 percent while the growth of urbanized land here grew by 236 percent. "Development" outstripped the growth in number of humans by a ratio of seventeen-to-one. The national average is three-to-one. We're gobbling land and hollowing out.

If we don't figure a new way to make it all work, this book is documenting a vanishing way of life, and you can file it with your histories of Carthage and Troy. Betsy and I already know that if we ever moved, we could not replicate the life we enjoy now.

Pirates and Steelers

I'm going to get into some graph-laden public policy before this book is done, so let me put a twist on a familiar moment in this football town. Let's have a half-time show. I'll invert the tradition and devote the intermission to the games. The real world and its numbers can wait a few pages.

David Hollander, the Mt. Lebanon native who created the CBS drama, *The Guardian,* drew heavily from our region's rough-around-the-edges nature to enrich that show. Hollander grew up in the 1970s and '80s when the Steelers and steel moved in opposite directions, and he was shaped by that time of "insularity, enormous civic pride and decay."

"The toughness of the people, the toughness of those kids," Hollander said. "If it isn't really the culture, it's the fantasy of the culture. The puffed-up chest, the big upper body, the skinny legs."

In the autumn of 2004 and early winter of 2005, chest-puffing was epidemic as the Steelers rolled through a fifteen-game win streak. By playoff time, a merely casual fan such as I could lose face to the sixty-something woman behind the counter at The Priory Bakery for not knowing who wore No. 22, one of the numbers featured on Steelers cookies that then were selling way better than hotcakes.

"That's the Duce," she told me incredulously. "Staley."

That Saturday, almost four of every five televisions in use in the Pittsburgh market were tuned to the overtime playoff victory over the New York (Psst—It's Really New Jersey) Jets. That TV rating would be Super Bowl-level for most cities. When the Steelers season came to an inglorious end the following Sunday before the biggest crowd in Heinz Field's young life, a front-page story in the *Post-Gazette* by Steve Levin and Robert Dvorchak caught the mood: "So much oxygen hadn't been sucked out of the North Side since the implosion of Three Rivers Stadium."

Redemption came the following year. In the five weeks leading up to the Super Bowl against the Seattle Seahawks in 2006, the *Post-Gazette* ran

Chad Garber convinced his wife, Laura, to paint her belly for Super Bowl XL in Detroit, February 5, 2006. Annie O'Neill, Pittsburgh Post-Gazette.

more than five hundred stories and photo captions containing the words "Steelers" and "Super Bowl." Detroit suddenly had the improbable allure of Shangra-La because that's where the big game would be.

Steeler Nation peacefully conquered that domed Detroit stadium, Terrible Towels waving by the thousands as the Steelers beat the Seahawks. Two days later, a quarter-million people squeezed Downtown for a victory parade. They overflowed into the streets. A friend and I tried to walk down Liberty Avenue for lunch on Market Square and were turned back by the civic equivalent of a goal-line stand. We couldn't get even as far as the Gateway Center subway stop, the love fest in black and gold being so wide and deep, but it did make for a nice cushion when Steelers safety Troy Polamalu did a mosh dive into fans' arms.

Three years later, Steelers Nation reprised the whole shebang. Tampa became Pittsburgh South for a long, loud, beer-fueled weekend and about 80 percent of the people in Raymond James stadium held a Terrible Towel in one hand that Sunday night as the Steelers pulled out a last-minute Super Bowl victory. Two days later, 350,000 made the big victory parade

Polamalu laying atop a wave of fans along the Boulevard of the Allies during the Super Bowl victory parade, 2009. Michael Henninger, Pittsburgh Post-Gazette.

and Polamalu did an even more spectacular jump from a car to 'Burghers' adoring arms for his encore.

"It's a divided city, not just by race and class and ethnicity, but by geography and topography, by hilltops and river valleys," Rob Ruck, this town's premier balls-and-bats historian, told *The New York Times* before that Jets game in 2005. "What unifies Pittsburgh more than anything are sports. Of any sport, it is the Steelers."

Why do we go nuts this way? A claim on the wall of Western Pennsylvania Sports History Museum puts the matter succinctly: "No city of comparable size has matched Pittsburgh's success in sport. Its teams have won more than a score of championships."

Notice the qualifier: "no city of comparable size." We look good partly because we shrunk. When the Pirates won their first World Series in 1909, there were only eight American cities larger than Pittsburgh, and now there are fifty-six.

Let's not quibble. The Steelers of 2004 helped lift a town badly in need of smiles, living as we were through a typically hard winter made worse by the city's and US Airways' money woes. Then the Steelers teams that followed allowed us to blow the dust off that "City of Champions" tag. If you want to understand Western Pennsylvania, you need to get to some games.

The Pirates

In the late summer of 1990, the Pirates were in a pennant race and a guy was in the emergency room in Sewickley Valley Hospital with blocked arteries. He'd been sick for two weeks, so his wife dragged him there, where he lay with a radio stuck in his ear, trying to get a score on the Mets-Cardinals game.

Doctor kept telling him he's a heart attack waiting to happen, and his teary wife was hanging on every word, but our man was thinking diamonds, not hearts.

"Don't worry about it now, Doc," Stanley Kon said. "The Mets are losing one-nothing, and the Pirates are winning."

Kon was seventy then, and had been a Pirates fan since he could hold a bat. As a teenager, he'd bum rides from Ambridge to Forbes Field. I found out about him because a co-worker happened to be on the other side of the cloth partition in the hospital.

"I had a bad heart," Kon told me, "but I had a live battery in that radio, thank heavens."

The retired steelworker enjoyed his summer evenings on his porch in West Aliquippa. That same July and August, when I walked through the South Side in what then remained an unyuppified zone in the Flats south of Carson, you'd hear the Pirates coming through the open row house windows of fans enjoying the cool of the evening. It was the first of three consecutive summers that the team won the division championship, only to be knocked out each successive autumn in the first round of the play-offs. The Pirates haven't had a winning year since that last excruciating loss to the Braves in Atlanta on October 14, 1992, The Night of Francisco Cabrera. (If that lyrical name brings you no sadness, ask no questions. You have led a blessed life.)

The French-born cultural historian Jacques Barzun once said that if you want to know the heart and mind of America, you must first understand baseball. Likewise, understanding Pittsburgh requires some study of our diametrical approaches to the Steelers and Pirates. After each team won its championship following the 1979 seasons, neither won another for more than a quarter-century. Nobody had any reason to believe in 1980 that we'd never see another championship again. But as the decades doubled, a decided split occurred. Everyone believed the Steelers would win the Super Bowl again, and almost nobody could see the Pirates in another World Series. Yet we'd watch them both, year after year, letting go of neither our hope nor our despair.

That's not to say the loves are equal. That has never been true in my time in Pittsburgh. In the summer of 1990, I moved to the North Side, chasing my boyhood dream of walking to major league games whenever the whim struck. Maybe that was a less a chase than an amble, but one Saturday night that August, I decided to go around the corner to a Western Avenue saloon to watch the big Pirates-Reds game from Cincinnati.

There are nights in this particular bar where you feel there should be a sign above the door, "Abandon Hope All Ye Who Enter Here." The usual crowd can be pretty thick with drooping heads. But when I walked in expecting to see the baseball game—the Reds were the team the Pirates soon would face in the playoffs—what I found instead was the first Steelers exhibition game. Every man in the place was transfixed, and that game did not come off until the last third-string quarterback had thrown his last incomplete pass for a team that would go nowhere that fall. Only then did I get to enjoy the glorious company of Barry Bonds, Andy Van Slyke and the rest of my beloved Pirates.

In the years since, that dichotomy has only grown. Baseball is a sport where big-money teams always have enjoyed a decided advantage, and that has been coupled with chronic incompetence in the Pirates organization. Or maybe it just hasn't cared enough about winning because it remains an enormously profitable business. Either way, rooting for the Pirates almost has become the love that dare not to speak its name. To go into a tavern in the early years of this century and ask the barkeep to turn on the Pirates game is to risk a look that says, "You poor, deluded, miserable man." Sixteen consecutive losing seasons represent a level of failure nearly unmatched in the history of American professional sports. And as I write, the Pirates seem a very good bet to set the all-time professional sports record for futility with a seventeenth consecutive losing season in 2009.

I remember one night, sitting in our parlor a few years ago. Betsy and the girls were soundly asleep upstairs and I was pondering how pathetic my pastime was. It could have been almost any spring or summer night since 1993, because the Pirates were blowing another lead in the eighth inning, and these two questions were running through my mind:

Question 1: Who is sadder, the two $1.5 million relief pitchers who couldn't find home plate with a flashlight, or me, the dork in the dark who isn't getting paid a dime to care, yet does?

Question 2: Are there any Iron City long necks left in the fridge?

The Pirates blew that game, one of more than sixteen hundred they've lost since I moved to Pittsburgh. Orlando Merced won it for the Houston Astros with a key base hit and a stolen base, which was pretty remarkable for a 107-year-old man. I assume Merced was past the century mark, because he played for the Pirates when Bonds did, which seems that long ago.

My brother, The Incredible Dullboy, visiting with his family one spring, sat with me in that same parlor as I paid way too much attention to the Pirates blowing another game another night. Dullboy told me I was obsessed.

Obsessed? What does he know? Dullboy roots for the Yankees, a team that needs to overpay cranky and fragile pitching aces just to taste some of the angst we Pirates fans accept as our due. What can Dullboy know about suffering?

The day after we lost the game to the 107-year-old man and his team named for the Jetsons' dog, I chastised myself for not kneeling down before bed to thank God that we have only basic cable, which keeps me from watching the Pirates on TV. Not everyone is so blessed. The Pirates in their losing years have averaged more than sixty thousand grimacing television viewers a game, which explains a lot about this town's enduring pessimism.

In the movie, *Field of Dreams*, James Earl Jones gives a speech in that Voice of God or The Phone Company way of his, wherein he speaks of the game's importance to our identity:

The one constant through all the years, Ray, has been baseball. America has rolled by like an army of steamrollers. It's been erased like a blackboard, rebuilt, and erased again. But baseball has marked the time. This field, this game, is a part of our past, Ray. It reminds us of all that once was good, and that could be again.

That may be a bit much, but don't underestimate the way mythic moments on fields of play form our identity. During my first decade or so in Pittsburgh, almost any lull in a Pirates game could be filled, almost any stranger at the ballpark could be engaged and befriended, simply by throwing out some woe at the injustice of Bill Mazeroski not being in the Hall of Fame. Maz, the greatest fielding second baseman who ever lived, stood for every hard-working stiff who ever did his job well but got no thanks for the powers that be.

"Why isn't Maz in the Hall?" someone would ask on the letters page of the Sports Section on another dreary Saturday in winter, and grown men and women across Western Pennsylvania would take long sips from their coffee, stare sadly into the gray morning light, and ask, indeed, "Why?"

It was the perfect Pittsburgh question. Mazeroski's absence from the Hall reinforced the essential irony of the Iron City outlook: Nothing ever changes in Pittsburgh and yet everything was somehow better before.

Each October 13th, hundreds of baseball fans assemble on the small patch of grass that still grows before the remnants of Forbes Field's ivy-covered brick outfield wall. They return to this holy ground to listen to an audiotape of the seventh game of the 1960 World Series, the game and the series that Mazeroski won by leading off the ninth inning with one of the most dramatic home runs in baseball history.

Every year since 1985, two or three hundred fans have gathered there on the sacred date, timing the taped broadcast so Maz hits the home run at precisely the same time he did in that last glorious autumn of the Eisenhower administration. Many, like me, are too young to have experienced the moment firsthand. Yet people straggle in with folding chairs and coolers of Iron City because, in the unreality of half-listening to an ancient contest whose outcome is known by heart, this folk event is more genuine than the slick shows that are part of the modern game. On the fortieth anniversary, the Pirate Parrot showed up and was booed simply for reminding people it was not 1960.

What made the day in 2000 magical was Mazeroski's appearance. On a bright, sunny day—strikingly like the afternoon exactly forty years before—the old man began signing autographs. Hats, shirts, old programs, anything that was handed to him, Mazeroski signed. Then the crowd went silent to hear the fateful final inning begin yet again. Then the home run was called. Then . . . euphoria!

Bill Mazeroski (left) and fans cheer his home run in the Pirates 1960 World Series victory over the Yankees. Mazeroski joined fans celebrating the fortieth anniversary of the win. Steve Mellon, Pittsburgh Post-Gazette.

Mazeroski soon made his way through the crowd and was slapped on the back by fans who had always wanted to slap that back, had always wanted to thank Maz, and now could in a time and place that made the experience new and nostalgic all at once.

"Only in Pittsburgh can something like this happen," former broadcaster Nellie King said that afternoon.

It's impossible to overestimate the hold the Maz moment has on a certain generation of Pittsburghers. In October 2002 I was walking down Sixth Street after working very late one night, and I heard the sound of a baseball game coming from a white Lexus convertible. Figuring it was that night's playoff game, I leaned over to ask the driver the score.

"Hal Smith just hit a three-run homer to put the Pirates ahead 9-7 over the Yankees in the 1960 World Series," the driver said.

The guy had a bootleg tape of the ancient seventh game. For Stan 'The Wine Man' Lalic, a wine importer from Brookline, the thrill is never gone. He slides that tape in, rolls down the top on his convertible, rides through his town, and he's a Little Leaguer watching the big game with his dad again.

"It's so vivid to me. I don't care if anyone else gets it. I get it."

The Pirates won two more World Series in the 1970s, each one also coming down to the last game and each providing its own sweet images, but none has diminished that magic moment in 1960 when Pittsburgh was still a big city and we seemed to have it all.

So when Maz finally was selected for the Hall in March 2001, four decades and change after he won the World Series, there was a sense of joy. But immediately behind it was an odd feeling of loss. The underdog had become an overachiever. A great unifier of the local sports fan disappeared. I remember thinking, "What are we going to gripe about now?"

The answer, of course, was "Just about everything." This is Pittsburgh, after all.

The Steelers

The Steelers, as I've said, are a different story altogether. Take the night in mid-December 1997, when Betsy was way pregnant with our first child. The in-laws were in town, down from Wisconsin's Northwoods. The Steelers were down by eight points with two minutes to go. The dinner reservation was 15 minutes away. Something had to give.

When I emerged from the bedroom with my jacket, I saw what that something would be. The TV was off. Coats were on. It was futile to resist the Cheeseheads. I could argue that a dinner reservation is not a plane reservation; the table wouldn't fly off without us. But Betsy had The Look. Jerome Bettis himself could not get past The Look.

The four of us walked to the car. It was parked in a lot a couple of blocks away because the neighborhood was holding its Victorian Christmas tour, and we, the people, had gotten our cars off the street for the weekend so the avenues could embrace the look of the century past. When twenty-two hundred strangers are willing to drop $17.50 apiece just to walk through a neighborhood doing a Currier & Ives impression, a two-minute stroll to your car isn't much to ask.

So we were walking these timeless streets as nearly everyone else within a one hundred-mile radius watched the Steelers send another game into overtime. We'd seen defensive end Kevin Henry's interception just before the TV went off, a grab that put the Steelers on the eighteen-yard line with two minutes to go, a touchdown and a two-point conversion needed to tie. I'm not a huge football fan, but this was a contest for the ages, and never mind that I can't remember today who the other team was. My father-in-law, a Green Bay Packers season-ticket holder, was as eager as I to get back to the game.

As we walked down Galveston Avenue, I looked into Fred Tait's barber shop. A neighborhood institution for more than two decades, Tait's is always busy, and has been favored over the years by Steelers and Pirates.

But at that point I'd never been inside. In America, barber shops are among the many quasi-public places that are either black or white, and Tait's is a black man's shop. As we were passing this night, though, everyone in Tait's had the look of one who'd just seen something great. I tried the door. It was locked, but then a man opened it to say the shop was closed.

"Did the Steelers tie it up?" I asked.

"21-21," he said over a broadening smile, and patrons behind him let a murmur of approval rumble through the shop.

My father-in-law and I gave a little "All right!" We got the same in return. And then we strode away to hear the Steelers win in overtime on the car radio. The late great radio color man, Myron Cope, he of the "yoi and double yoi," summed it up as only he could. For a moment, the world seemed right.

I'd think about that later. Think about how this joyous moment occurred only a few hours after racially charged news had rolled across the TV screen: The jury trying two suburban police officers in the killing of Jonny E. Gammage, a black man pulled over in a traffic stop, could not reach a verdict. Another mistrial. Eleven white jurors had decided the white officers were not guilty of involuntary manslaughter; the lone black juror had seen the same evidence and decided they were.

The Steelers unite blacks and whites in this town like nothing else. They're a civic treasure.

The Steelers unite blacks and whites in this town like nothing else. Is that not a shame?

I did get my hair cut in Tait's about six months after that night. By then, our daughter Curran had been born and I took a few months paternity leave after Betsy went back to working for pay. I'd push Curran in her

Fred Tait. Photo by Larry Rippel.

stroller to the hospital each morning to see her mom and get her nourishment, nutritional and spiritual, and then I'd read the newspaper beside Lake Elizabeth in the park while Curran napped. I'd also take wider strolls with my girl, circling the block and the neighborhood, and so I got to know Aaron, who then worked the second chair at Tait's.

I hadn't known any barbers named Aaron; in most of the shops I'd visited, the second chair was manned by a Tony or a Nick. But Aaron and I would talk sports or kids or the weather, and one day I asked him if he could cut my hair.

"I can cut any kind of hair," he said.

So I went in, sat in his chair when my turn came, flipped through a magazine and talked. I've since gotten my hair cut by Fred, too, but on this day that Aaron had the scissors, a Herbie Hancock tune was playing. What I don't know about Hancock's music could fill this book, but it sounded good. I said as much and Aaron, in way of reciprocation, said, "You know whose music I really used to like? Edgar Winter."

Winter is an albino. I smiled inwardly because I had the sense that Aaron had reached for the whitest musician he could remember as a way of making me feel welcome. And it worked. Most of us here don't bother to risk even that much, and that's our loss.

The Penguins

What I don't know about hockey also could fill this book, but I went to a number of games in the early '90s, when my cousin Jim Monahan introduced me to the magic of Mario Lemieux. The game never snared me, though in some ways, I wish it had. The Penguins and their fans have a different kind of relationship, more familial than reverential. That was made apparent when they first won the Stanley Cup in 1991.

Imagine this. You're a Penguins fan. It's dawn on a Sunday in May. You are among the thousands who drove to the old airport to meet the heroes' plane, and now you are among the overflow crowd at the Eat 'n Park on Beers School Road, drooping through a daybreak breakfast. That's when you notice that a couple of guys have just walked in with the Stanley Cup.

For a moment, you think you're seeing things, that someone spiked your orange juice, but no. That's it. That's the Cup, the Cup, THE STANLEY CUP!

"I could have locked it in the car," Rick Paterson, the Pens' assistant coach, said later. "But people deserve to see it. They went through a lot of agony here."

For the Shadows, a dek hockey team from Castle Shannon, the chance to hold the championship trophy turned that night around. Remembering the reaction, Paterson said, "They wanted to be around it like it was a living thing."

By 1 p.m. that Sunday, Paterson had it on his front lawn in Franklin Park. Neighbors arrived with beer and champagne, and then took turns drinking from it. That night, Paterson and trainer Skip Thayer took the Cup down the road to Carmody's restaurant.

"You could not get a telephone in that restaurant," Mike Carmody said. "People were leaving in cars and bringing people back."

Thayer took it home to Evans City from there. It spawned a traffic jam when he put it on his lawn the next day, Memorial Day. Ron Francis, a

Penguins center, told Paterson he went to a Ross Park Mall film store on Memorial Day and he saw them rolling off pictures of the Cup on Paterson's lawn.

The Cup had taken twenty-four years to get to Pittsburgh, but it made itself at home in no time. For something named for a lord, the trophy sure knew how to mingle. But that's the kind of town this is. Even the name of The Cup had to be taken down a peg by some, given the same nickname Eastern Europeans used to give to Stanleys hereabouts. A friend told me, "This is Pittsburgh. It's time to drop the formalities and call it 'The Stosh Cup.'"

Penguins fans still packed the Mellon Arena for the 2005-'06 season, even with the team stinking on ice and Mario making all kinds of noise about selling and moving the Pens. They packed it again in 2006-'07, as a young team led by a new Canadian superstar, Sidney Crosby, sent the team toward the playoffs even as Mario made a show of moving the team to Kansas City.

Remember that schmaltzy proverb from the '70s? "If you love something, set it free. If it comes back, it's yours. If it doesn't, it never was meant to be." Penguins fans epitomized that sentiment. Mario could tell fans he was taking their beloved team to a smaller metropolitan area with a weaker TV market and a bad hockey history, and Pittsburgh fans, from one of the most loyal American outposts of what is a fourth-rung sport nearly everywhere else, told him to take the best deal he could get. Once the Penguins tied the idea of a Pittsburgh slots casino to financing a new hockey arena, that stuck like fries to melted cheese. All the pressure to compromise was put on politicians, and Governor Ed Rendell finally gave the Penguins a ridiculously good deal on a new ice house.

After that deal was announced at a Pens game in March 2007, a packed house gave Mario a standing ovation in the arena they all deride, believing he had saved Pittsburgh hockey. But only a fool would have passed on that deal, and Mario is no fool. The most gifted athlete ever to play for this town may be an even greater businessman. The people these fans should have cheered are Amish farmers in Lancaster County, waitresses in Philadelphia, bus drivers in Scranton and all the losers who will pack that casino hard by the West End Bridge, which is pledged to cough up $7.5 million each year for thirty years, a figure the state will match with its own slots revenue, to build the new arena. The Penguins need put up only $4.2

million a year.

There is no parallel for this in sports. It's as if Willie Mays were trying to move the Giants from New York to San Francisco in the 1950s and all those tough New Yorkers just said: "Aw, Willie, just do what you gotta do."

The region's mass transit system happened to be pretty strapped at the time and couldn't muster any state help, but as a friend told me, "Nobody ever gave a standing ovation for the arrival of the 77B."

If you step back from the ice you can understand this. Pens fans' unparalleled loyalty is a by-product of living in a place with too much of the not-there-anymores. Remember the only task Pittsburgh has is to keep the good stuff that's already here. For some that might be the opera, the symphony, their church or the Dormont Pool. For these fans, some among them those same kids from the Castle Shannon team who reached out to touch the Stanley Cup the morning it stopped at Eat 'n Park a half-lifetime before, it most definitely is Penguins hockey.

In the spring of 2009, Penguins fans were rewarded with another Stanley Cup. Their team won a dramatic seventh game from the Red Wings in Detroit, the first professional team to win the seventh game of a championship on the road since the Pirates beat the Orioles in Baltimore in 1979. The big silver cup bopped around the old town again that weekend, showing up everywhere from the night clubs of East Carson Street to the diamond of PNC Park, and then 375,000 fans turned out for the biggest victory parade that Pittsburgh had seen in, well, about four months.

Penguins fans won. How many of the rest of us will?

Coming Home

Lawrenceville: the Land the Chains Forgot. Penn Avenue, 2004. Darrell Sapp, Pittsburgh Post-Gazette.

Tom Purcell came home. Purcell was part of the Pittsburgh diaspora that spawned the epidemic of Steelers bars across America and helped make the *Post-Gazette* Web site, www.post-gazette.com, the 25th most popular newspaper site in 2008, while the folding newspaper's circulation ranked only 42nd. About two-thirds of the *PG's* online readers don't live in the region. Ex-'Burghers stay tuned to the hometown through cyberspace.

Leaving the region in the late 1990s for Washington D.C., Purcell easily found work in marketing and communications. Out there, he says, "One in five people is from Pittsburgh and they all want to come back.

But they can't."

He's exaggerating, but there are thousands of black-and-gold nomads in and around Washington. They needn't wear the colors to stand out. Unlike most of the drones in the nation's capital, Purcell says, "they're demonstrative. They have facial expressions. They're outward. They make eye contact.

"This is a very human place," he told me as we had coffee one Saturday morning in January at Uptown Coffee in Mt. Lebanon, south of the city, after he'd moved back. "This is the way people are supposed to be."

He returned when he figured out some things.

1. His kind of writing can be done anywhere.

2. The condo he bought in Mt. Lebo for $48,000 would easily cost four times that in Northern Virginia. "You can't buy a one-bedroom condominium in the whole D.C. area for less than $200,000."

3. "Everything I hated about Pittsburgh is exactly the same thing I now love."

Purcell grew up in Bethel Park at the tail end of the baby boom in the '60s and '70s, the third of six children, and went on to major in English at Penn State. In more than two decades since graduation, he has done everything from stand-up comedy to penning a mystery novel (set in Pittsburgh, of course.) At first he was grateful for the anonymity he had in Washington—"I didn't have to shower"—but he ultimately missed the connectedness he has here.

About the time we talked, we had a story in the *PG* about "third places," the diners, bars and coffee shops from Aspinwall to Zelienople that provide a sense of community. Sociologist Ray Oldenburg coined the term in his book, *The Great Good Place*. The design of the post-war suburb left little room for them, Oldenburg lamented.

"More and more, our lives are divided between an alienated workplace and a private home, with only a torturous commute to mediate," he wrote. "A third place, the great good place, is sadly disappearing."

"In Northern Virginia," said Purcell, "there are no such places as the pubs that are *all* over Pittsburgh. People get in their cars to drive to a giant parking lot to meet at Starbucks, but that's about it. We have a piece of heaven here right under our noses."

He's setting his mystery novel inside a warm, cozy pub on the South Side. An ex-Pittsburgh cop owns the joint, still fighting crime when he's not pouring *Arns* (the local term for Iron City beer).

"I strongly believe people are *longing* for these kinds of connections," Purcell said. "It's the old *Cheers* thing. One of the reasons that show was so successful was the sense of camaraderie and friendship that takes the edge off the fast pace we have now."

On the morning we met for coffee, Purcell desperately needed the java jolt, having just spent a night on the town with his cousins. These guys, he said, have gotten in fights at three of the last five weddings.

Three of the last five?

Purcell thought about it again, and saw fit to correct himself.

"Three of the last four."

Being part of an extended family again, being in a place where people look out for you and forgive your quirks is something he now appreciates. He told of walking through the Strip District and a stranger telling him his wallet was falling out of his back pocket. When he told the stranger he just had a high wallet, the man pointed to the dollar bills poking out.

"Flip it a-rond," he said. When Purcell started to walk away, the man became more adamant: "Flip it A-ROND!"

Purcell flipped his wallet around, bills down in his pocket. Nothing less would have satisfied the stranger.

"He's outward. That would never happen in most places on the planet. Walking down the street [in Washington], people will not look at you."

But there's also negativity and a resistance to change here that frustrates him. Provincialism can be either charming or damning depending on how it strikes you on any given day. Pittsburgh should find a way to market itself to people like Tom and perhaps concede the twentysomethings to places like Austin, Seattle and New York. Young, educated Americans are footloose by nature; they're going to head for bright lights or beaches. But once they've been there and done that, many look homeward.

Tereneh Mosley was one of those "boomerang people." She returned in 2002 after fifteen years away in Philadelphia, New York, Seattle and Chicago, picking up on an excitement and energy during a Thanksgiving visit that she hadn't seen before. The trick, she said then, is not telling people about Pittsburgh, it's getting them to visit. You might look at a puppy in a window and keep walking, she said, but if you go in and hold it, you're going to buy it.

But here's where the story turns because Tereneh Mosley would not stay.

She'll tell you she has been shaped by our culture: classical music, jazz, Pittsburgh Ballet Theater, the plays of August Wilson, the Carnegie museums and, not least, the art of her father, the sculptor Thad Mosley. She says she went to "the best school on the planet," The Falk School, a laboratory school of the University of Pittsburgh. It turned out an eclectic group of people she still calls friends. And all that is leavened with the blue-collar work ethic the city gave her, which has served her well from New York to Milan to Nairobi. And yet. And yet.

"Pittsburgh does not want me to be cool. And you know what? That is just fine with me."

Since her return, her hopes for the city have been dashed by a young mayor she doesn't think is up to the job, "a casino on the banks of the sacred Ohio," a big UPMC sign tarnishing the stark dignity of the US Steel Tower and the rigidity of local thinking. Most friends from her Falk days have moved away.

"Pittsburgh wants to keep their provincial mind-set with ethnic groups and races hunkered down in separate bunkers? Again, cool, where's my shovel? I get asked to pull my Afro hair back in some 'professional' settings and I have to order hair products online because it so darn hard to find natural hair products for long Afro hair like mine in Pittsburgh. Seems like a small deal. Nope. I am a girl and hair is major.

"I like to go out a lot. I want to explore places I have yet to go. But no matter who I ask, the same half-dozen nightspots pop up.

"I realized I want progressive, smart leadership. I want a beautiful sky-line, not a billboard in the heavens. I do not like gambling. I hate bunkers. I like people of all races. I love my Afro and my Afro likes to go to new places, new nightspots, maybe even meet another cool big Afro.

"For the past twenty years, since I left high school, I have spent only three years in Pittsburgh. It is where I am from but it is not where I am at—to almost quote [rapper] Mos Def. I have done a lot to try to 'change' Pittsburgh—boards, activities and more. However, Pittsburgh has made it clear what it wants to be and that does not include me."

I'm a chronically unhip, white, graying father of grade-schoolers, but I know what Tereneh means. You don't need Afro anxiety to know what Tereneh means. When I began this book, my working title was *I Love Pittsburgh Like a Brother—and My Brother Drives Me Nuts.* Anyone living here any length of time can work up a solid love/hate page, and it's pretty clear thousands have found enough on the wrong side of that ledger to flee. My concerns are decidedly more wonkish than Tereneh's, and I'll be laying them on fairly thick in the next few chapters. But what drew Tereneh back in the first place (and what I hope will, one day, draw her back yet) is that hometown, "puppy dog," comfort. That's where Pittsburgh has a true edge—if you can find a place to work.

Will Drosendahl is a senior software consultant more than twenty years past graduation from Syracuse University. He lives in Ross. He used to work Downtown, and then from home, but he changed jobs and now reports to an office in Raleigh, North Carolina.

"Here's the crazy part," he told me not long after he got that Carolina job. "I have never been to those main offices. I work from home. I currently *am* the Pittsburgh office, and my nearest colleagues are in Boston and Michigan. It seems a bit odd to figuratively follow in the footsteps of former Pittsburghers who went to Raleigh to seek employment while my only move was to swap laptops."

Drosendahl since has been to Raleigh, and his job also takes him to England. His company is global, with clients in Tokyo and staffers in India, so he keeps five time zones marked on a wallboard at his home in Ross.

I don't know enough about the computer industry or marketing to know how to find more people like Tom and Will, but finding even a few thousand more folks who can pull their paychecks from somewhere else and spend them here would be good. Advertise on a Web site where techies go and ask who wants to live in a 3,000 square foot house that costs only X. We may be surprised who shows up.

They won't necessarily be techies. In the summer of 1998, Bob Barone, a reserved, retired English teacher, and his wife, Loretta, an exuberant, effusive yoga teacher, moved against the tide of American retirements and became rust birds, selling their little house in Coral Gables, Florida, and buying a bigger brick one in Point Breeze for less money.

"The storm we had, Brian, it was heaven," Mrs. Barone told me that winter, shrugging off a slip on the ice that left her wrist with a hairline fracture but did nothing to shake her fondness for her adopted town.

The Barones came for the symphony, the opera, the four seasons, and a safe, affordable urban neighborhood. Many years after their move they continue to behave like "a couple of dopey kids," finding short cuts through Polish Hill most natives don't know and just generally digging the scene.

"Wherever we go, we'll just look at each other, grinning from ear to ear," she said of their drives. "But somebody really needs to coordinate the stoplights and do something about the potholes."

I didn't say love was blind.

Bob and Mary Hartley moved to Lawrenceville a decade ago because "we picked Pittsburgh off the map as the city we wanted to live in." She told me that one winter day in 1997, when she still had an antique shop on Butler Street. A stereo had Ella Fitzgerald singing about heaven, and Mary was nearly doing the same.

"Ultimately, we'd like to have kids and raise them in a city, and this is certainly one of the safest cities in America."

I've met a number of Chicago expatriates here, and recent arrivals from bigger cities often have a three-part reaction as they begin kicking around the 'Burgh, which goes something like: Holy cow; this is cool; where is everyone? These folks often settle in neighborhoods that natives largely have written off, then get on the phone and brag about the deal to families back home.

The Hartleys' neighborhood, Lawrenceville, begins a couple of miles east of Downtown, stretches along the Allegheny River for a couple more, and has a history nearly as long as Pittsburgh itself. Stephen Foster's old man, who had his son's gift for catching the American ear, established the village in 1814 and named it for Captain James Lawrence, a hero of the War of 1812, famous for his dying words, "Don't Give up the Ship!" Whether or not it was due to that timely marketing hook, Lawrenceville took off. It was absorbed by the city a few years after the Civil War, but never lost its name, its identity or its allure to pioneers of one form or another.

A steady exodus of residents began well before the collapse of steel and continued through the 1990s, but by then newcomers had begun to see the value in solid old homes close to Downtown and the university-hospital complex. Incomers didn't outnumber outgoers, which kept homes affordable. The Hartleys bought a four-bedroom 1890 house, with a two-car garage and a front porch on Main Street in Lawrenceville in the summer of 1996. It cost them $350 a month, about what a studio apartment in Chicago had cost seven years before. Such are the deals you can wangle when you move to a neighborhood that has lost two-thirds of its population since 1940.

They sold the home they bought for $40,000 three years later for

$60,000. It now could be worth twice that. As Americans opt for larger homes and smaller families than their moms and dads, a neighborhood can be revitalized with far fewer residents than generations past. The Hartleys have stayed in Lawrenceville, buying a brick home on nearly an acre of land with twenty mature trees. Theirs is only the second family in that home since 1880. It is there that their son Jack and daughter Gracie play.

The Hartleys also bought a building on Butler Street, Lawrenceville's commercial corridor that has echoed Carson Street's '80s and '90s revival on the South Side. In the fall of 2007, *The New York Times* rightly cheered Butler Street for being "the place the chain stores forgot," making room instead for galleries, boutiques and funky shops.[8]

When Mary left the antique business, the Hartleys leased the place to an ad agency, which proved another great choice. Not that bricks and mortar are everything. "We came for the house but stayed for the neighbors," she says, quoting a friend.

Bob Hartley is now a respiratory therapist, making a reverse commute to UPMC Passavant in the North Hills, and Mary has taken a job with The Arc of Greater Pittsburgh, helping people with disabilities get dental care.

The oft-maligned city schools have been a godsend. The best school for their older child Jack and his high-functioning autism is Martin Luther King Elementary on the North Side, where he attends class with seven or eight other children. His teacher, Danielle Frye, is so dedicated "she probably dreams about teaching," Mary said.

Of course, Lawrenceville ain't Mt. Lebanon. In a neighborhood where a bar with a "no teeth, no service" sign only recently disappeared, they expect to set stricter ground rules than some have. They'll be no "hanging out" on the streets. When the time comes, they expect to allow their children to take a bus or walk to a museum, a ballgame, the library or the Boys & Girls Club, but they'll be required to come right back. It should be noticed that those rules would not be much different in the suburbs, though there'd be fewer walkable destinations.

Buying the house the Hartleys did for what they paid, three miles from Downtown? "You still can't do that in any other city in America." She credits all the families who stuck it out through tough times, keeping Lawrenceville a special place, and now jokes about "the Hep Cat Factor," counting all the people she sees around now who are "cooler and younger than me" and giving the neighborhood Giant Eagle a reason to open a small organic food section.

She sees potential in other neglected parts of the city. She knows the views from Allentown and the convenience of the Hill District and Uptown, but too few are with her. There is, she says, "a haze of negativity over this city. It starts to get in your gut."

Beth Zak, and her husband, Mike, also moved here from Chicago, but she was coming home. She's Will Drosendahl's younger sister. When I asked what would make them leave their jobs in his hometown, they talked about the traffic, the congested streets and parks and the "crazy, crazy money" it took to buy a decent house in Chicago. That city had seemed great when they met in their twenties, almost an extension of college life with young transplants swarming every tall apartment building and nightspot. But the world looks a little different once you hit your thirties. In 2004, Beth got word that her best friend from childhood had died. He also had lived in Chicago, but moved back to Pittsburgh near the end of his life to be with his parents and receive treatment for melanoma from UPMC. Soon after, the Zaks decided they would not move to the Chicago suburbs. Instead, they sold their home in Chicago and moved to her parents' home in Shaler. They'd look for work in Pittsburgh. Life is too short to spend it someplace you no longer want to be.

Few have the guts to chuck everything and move without prospects, and as the months dragged on without work in a tough job market, the Zaks wondered if they'd made a mistake. But each eventually found work, he in Churchill and she out by the airport. When we spoke early in 2005, they were looking for a house somewhere in the middle, on the I-279 corridor, and marveling just how open everything seems, from the parkways to the bike trails. They ultimately bought a home in the North Hills.

Are these people trendsetters, putting family and roots ahead of financial "success"? We need to hope so. Pittsburgh needs their energy. Pennsylvania long has benefited from people who could see its potential with fresh eyes, starting with William Penn and Ben Franklin. Andy Carnegie, George Westinghouse and maybe your grandma all came from somewhere else to leave their mark here. Pittsburgh started slipping when that slowed down.

I Love Pittsburgh Like a Brother
(and My Brother Drives Me Nuts)

Nearly all that came before this makes me love Pittsburgh like a brother. Now here's why my brother drives me nuts.

Like Big Steel and US Airways, which did not respond to their competitors' moves until they were not just on the ropes but under the ring, our city and state are playing by rules exactly wrong for the twenty-first century. They've been wrong for generations, but you have to go back a century or so to see why.

The U.S. Census of 1910 was the first to find Pittsburgh as one of America's ten largest cities. Three years before, Pittsburgh had swallowed the City of Allegheny whole, giving this new appendage the utilitarian name "North Side," against the smaller city's will. That annexation, which became official in December 1907, was big; it represented the merger of the nation's eleventh and twenty-seventh largest cities. But it wasn't revolutionary. Allegheny had itself swallowed the smaller community of Manchester years before. Pittsburgh had grown from less than two square miles to nearly thirty in the decade following the Civil War by annexing the boroughs of Lawrenceville, Mt. Washington and other smaller towns. Such moves made sense as Pittsburgh's economy became more complex. Annexation remains commonplace in America's Sun Belt but, in Pennsylvania, it's history. Because after the city annexed Allegheny in 1907, small-town interest groups banded together and changed the state constitution to make such moves all but impossible.[9]

Even back then, people worried Pittsburgh was falling behind. In 1923, the governor appointed a commission with representatives from all the county municipalities. The idea was to create one federated city. The commission pushed an amendment to the state constitution through Harrisburg with the goal of making our county-turned-city the fourth largest city in America.[10]

Voters statewide approved the constitutional amendment, and the state General Assembly chiseled a charter for this new kind of city, one in which all existing municipalities would remain intact. People must have liked it because in June 1929, fully 68 percent of the county approved the charter. Approval was widespread, with 82 of the 123 municipalities then in existence giving the OK.[11]

So why didn't it happen? Where's the federated city?

Hey, this is Pennsylvania, with an oversized state legislature fully capable of getting in its own way when it isn't having its own way. Somehow, it had written the bill so that it required two-thirds approval in a majority of the communities. It got that overwhelming support in only fifty of the 123. Nobody was even sure if the Legislature had set it up this way on purpose. The commission chairman blamed the bill's language on the printer.

Whether it was due to statehouse skullduggery or incompetence (that always has been a tough call in Harrisburg), minority ruled. Whatever chance Pittsburgh had of staying a big-time city died.[12] The law today is the same as then. Here in Pennsylvania, unlike the parts of America where cities grow, no small municipality can be annexed without a majority of its citizens voting for the change. Like that or not, that's the biggest reason all Pennsylvania cities are shrinking.

The Pittsburgh of 1910 had nearly 534,000 residents, the eighth largest population in the country. The city would peak four decades later with 676,806 residents, but would slip from the Top Ten (to twelfth) in that same 1950 Census. Pittsburgh was also slipping in proportion to Allegheny County, which would grow for another ten years. That was typical in post-war America.

"By 1950, New York City, Chicago and Philadelphia and many smaller cities had all stopped growing," Witold Rybczynski wrote in *City Life: Urban Expectations in a New World*. "Not that the metropolitan regions surrounding these cities were not vigorous, but 1950 is probably as good a date as any to mark the end—or more accurately, the beginning of the end—of traditional, concentrated cities."

The current metropolitan set-up is almost wholly dependent on cheap gasoline. The density of America's central cities dropped from 7,517 people per square mile to 2,716 in the last fifty years of the twentieth century.[13] That was not just because people left for the suburbs, or because families became smaller, but because the growing cities of the Sun Belt never have been packed tightly. Unlike the cities that boomed in the nineteenth and early twentieth centuries, these places are as auto-centric as Pittsburgh's suburbs. As Americans move farther from their workplaces, these new cities extend their borders to keep them. They annex their suburbs, making residents out of commuters, whether they like it or not. That's a key difference many Pennsylvanians don't see or don't want to see.

An easy way to show that is to compare the Top Ten cities of 1910 to the current Top Ten.

A century ago, only the three most populous cities—New York, Chicago and Philadelphia—covered more than one hundred square miles. The next seven averaged forty-three square miles, ranging from Baltimore's thirty to St. Louis's sixty-one. These densely packed places all had at least ten thousand residents per square mile in 1910.

There is no such big little city today. None. The only four cities from the old Top Ten that remained when the twenty-first century opened were those

America's Ten Most Populous Cities (sq. mi.)			
1910		**2000**	
New York	287	New York	303
Chicago	185	Los Angeles	469
Philadelphia	130	Chicago	227
St. Louis	61	Houston	579
Boston	41	Philadelphia	135
Cleveland	46	Phoenix	475
Baltimore	30	San Diego	324
Pittsburgh	41	Dallas	343
Detroit	41	San Antonio	408
Buffalo	39	Detroit	139

Square miles of the top ten cities of 1910 compared to the 2000 top ten. Source: U.S. Bureau of the Census.

covering at least one hundred square miles: New York, Chicago, Philadelphia and Detroit. Detroit more than tripled its square miles as the auto age made its sputtering beginnings, joining its larger cousins in the 100 square mile-club by 1930.

The other six cities have fallen, some of them hard. By 2006, St. Louis had dropped from fourth to fifty-second, Pittsburgh from eighth to fifty-seventh, Buffalo from tenth to sixty-sixth. All three had peaked in 1950.

Among America's one hundred largest cities, only St. Louis, Baltimore, Buffalo and Norfolk lost a larger percentage of their people than Pittsburgh in the '90s. Then came news early in 2007 that our seven-county region was second in recent population loss only to New Orleans, which was suffering the nearly biblical devastation of Hurricane Katrina.

We're off in a rust-belt corner with these little-box losers, all of which have kept pretty close to their old boundaries with predictably dismal results. Urban boundaries of the early twentieth century do not fit the auto age. As former Albuquerque mayor David Rusk put it, the American municipal equation is this simple: fixed-boundary cities and boroughs = population loss.

Scanning America's Top Ten in the 2000 Census, the smallest city in land area was Philadelphia, which merged with its surrounding county in 1854, before the age of trains fully arrived. No other top city is smaller than Philadelphia's 135 square miles (roughly two and one-half times the size of Pittsburgh.) The average is 340 square miles (roughly six times the size of Pittsburgh).

Why does that matter? Simple. If your city was built out to its borders before the auto age arrived, there was no good place in your city to build the malls and detached single-family homes that most people wanted by 1960. There was no way to expand your tax base unless your city's borders moved. Most of today's biggest cities spent the past century expanding their borders. They broadened their tax base to include those who live in the "real" Houston, San Diego or Phoenix, not just those within horse-and-buggy boundaries.

Houston went from seventeen square miles in 1910 to one hundred sixty square miles at mid-century to 579 square miles at century's end. San Diego has more than tripled its land area since mid-century, as has Dallas. San Antonio is nearly six times its 1950 land area. Phoenix is more than twenty-seven times its mid-century form. Mayors of these cities don't have

Land Expansion of the Ten Largest American Cities (sq. mi.)			
	1910	1950	2000	% Inc.
New York	286.8	315.1	303.3	6
Los Angeles	99.2	450.9	469.1	472
Chicago	185.1	207.5	227.2	23
Houston	17.4	160.0	579.4	3329
Philadelphia	130.2	127.2	135.1	4
Phoenix	N/A	17.1	474.9	2677
San Diego	N/A	99.4	324.3	226
Dallas	16.2	112.0	342.5	2014
San Antonio	35.8	69.5	407.6	1039
Detroit	40.8	139.6	138.8	240

Note: All percentage increases are from 1910 to 2000 with exceptions of Phoenix and San Diego, which are from 1950 to 2000. Neither Phoenix nor San Diego was among the nation's one hundred largest cities in 1910. Pittsburgh grew from 41.4 square miles in 1910 to 54.2 square miles in 1950 to 55.6 square miles in 2000. That's an increase of 34% since 1910 and less than 3% since 1950. Source: U.S. Bureau of the Census.

to lose sleep wondering whether people are shopping within a few blocks or even a few miles of city hall. Land gained by both Phoenix and San Antonio in the 1990s alone represents an area larger than Pittsburgh.

Even New York, which springs to most American minds when they think City with a capital C, benefited from a timely annexation. In 1898, New York annexed Brooklyn, Queens, the Bronx and Staten Island. Those last three boroughs were largely rural a century ago. My father, born in 1910, recalled farms in the Bronx of his youth. In 1900, there were more than two thousand farms within the confines of New York City.[14]

So Manhattan has lost a third of its population since it peaked in 1910, Brooklyn has dropped a tenth from its peak in 1950, and the Bronx has fallen similarly since peaking in 1970. So what? The combined population of the outer boroughs, Queens and Staten Island, has risen twelve-fold in the past century. With these quasi-suburban choices within its borders, offering malls and single-family tract housing, New York was able to surpass 8 million residents for the first time in 2000. Yet it is far less densely populated than when all its residents squeezed on the island of Manhattan.

My late father's story reflects that of his native city. Born in Manhattan, he moved with his family to the Bronx even before the subways stretched that far north. When the Bronx-Whitestone Bridge opened in 1939 in conjunction with the World's Fair in Queens, the O'Neills bought a house in Queens. A million people followed in succeeding decades. And when the Verrazano Narrows Bridge connected Brooklyn with Staten Island in 1964, the population of the city's last semi-rural borough exploded. Staten Island alone has more people than Pittsburgh now.

Now think about our city's story. It was pretty much out of elbow room by World War II. New homes were built in neighborhoods such as Banksville, Beechview, Brookline, Crafton Heights, Lincoln Place, Stanton Heights, Squirrel Hill, Swisshelm Park and Westwood in the 1950s, but that doesn't add up to much by modern urban standards. When these neighborhoods were done, so was the city. Almost every major highway built since World War II has leveled urban homes and businesses and encouraged moves to the suburbs. That is a national story, but governments in much of the rest of America have broadened their urban borders to deal with the new reality. Not Pennsylvania.

According to a U.S. Census Bureau survey, in the 1980s, 75,571 annexations occurred in the United States, involving 9,186 square miles and a population of nearly 2.6 million. During those same ten years, eighteen annexations occurred in Pennsylvania, involving less than one square mile and fewer than five hundred persons.[15]

Before World War II, about a quarter of the homes going up in the metro area were built in Pittsburgh. Since then, the percentage of new homes built in the city has dropped steadily. Heroic efforts to build on slag heaps and transform old factories and ill-conceived new department stores into trendy lofts notwithstanding, we have a city where more than half the homes were built by 1939, and nearly four of five by 1960.

That leaves no good place for a mall either. A half-century ago, Pittsburgh made square-peg-in-round-hole tries such as Allegheny Center on the North Side and the pedestrian mall in East Liberty, but neither could compete with true malls just outside the city limits. SouthSide Works has gotten off to a strong start with its upscale strategy, but Ross Park Mall, Monroeville Mall, Robinson Town Centre, South Hills Village—they're all closer to the Golden Triangle than outer-borough malls in New York City are to Manhattan, but all are equally meaningless to Pittsburgh's bottom line.

Pennsylvania was able to get away with this set-up as long as we had a manufacturing economy, but when America moved to a service economy, the state's cities began keeling over, the smallest ones first. Former Mayor Tom Murphy spent most of the 1990s saying that our hospitals and universities would be the "steel mills of the future," but that's not so and can never be so. These institutions generate tens of thousands of jobs, but the primary engines of the regional economy don't pay property or business taxes, and many a high-paid employee lives out of town, paying and generating taxes somewhere else.

That does not excuse the cities for their own sins. No absolution can be granted for those. Cities such as Pittsburgh have been going broke for at least thirty years, but until very recently have been acting as if they still had money. Only in past few years has real reform come, but that's still not enough.

When I lived around the Blue Ridge Mountains of Virginia, I once heard a joke that seems to fit here. An old codger picks up a hitchhiker and when the two men are motoring along, the codger tells the younger man to open the glove compartment. Hitchhiker sees a bottle of moonshine in there. Driver tells him to take a drink. Hitchhiker says he doesn't care for any. Codger pulls a gun.

"I said, take a drink.'"

So the young fellow takes a drink and it's awful stuff, just awful, burns all the way down and goes right to his head.

"OK," says the old man, handing the kid the gun. "Now make me take a drink."

Only with the state putting a gun to City Council's head in 2004 did the city make massive cuts in spending. That was a gun Mayor Murphy and City Council asked to be pointed at them, and the Democratic Council still wobbled under pressure from the firefighters union and others to the last moment.

Likewise, the Republican Legislature didn't go for the gun it bought.

It organized its own financial oversight committee to provide the political cover to do the right thing. But when this oversight committee said the city could not survive without restructuring business taxes and increasing the ten dollar annual occupation tax that hadn't moved since 1965, these legislators balked. They cut the proposed occupation tax increase in half, from $104 a year to $52. The higher number was indeed too much too soon, but cutting it in half meant this increase didn't even match inflation. (Ten dollars in 1965 would be worth about $63 in 2006.) It would have made more sense to have a tax that was some tiny percentage, perhaps one-tenth of one percent, rather than a one-size-fits-all tax, but at least this was some small recognition that the Pittsburgh metropolis has metropolitan needs. Trouble was America's Largest Full-Time State Legislature managed to write the law in a way that made it a "Kick Me" sign for Pennsylvania workers.

The change in the occupation tax was supposed to be only a buck a week, and wasn't supposed to affect people making less than $12,000 a year. But the language that would have spread the payments was inexplicably removed from the bill. (Funny how that sort of stuff keeps happening.)

Instead of a weekly charge that would be no more than Beaver Cleaver's allowance, the new state law had cities taking the full annual amount from paychecks in the first month of employment. That meant $52 in January, the very month that people face credit card bills so large they're cursing Santa.

Every worker had to pay the full load, even those at the minimum wage. Imagine working at McDonald's and seeing most of your paycheck disappear one very cold payday. Those earning less than twelve grand in the city were instructed to apply for their $42 rebates at the end of the tax year. In some places, such as West Mifflin, the threshold for payment began even lower. Kennywood amusement park's temporary workers were fleeced of the $52 in their first paychecks of summer.

Sorry, suckers—that was Pennsylvania's welcome to the working world.

The Legislature let this go for two consecutive Januaries until, late in 2006, it passed a bill to change the system to a buck a week—everywhere but in Pittsburgh. The city successfully argued to the right people in Harrisburg that its distressed status should allow it to keep holding up workers by their ankles and shaking fifty-two bucks from a single paycheck. Soon enough, other communities persuaded Governor Ed Rendell to veto the reform entirely, and the same Legislature that had been for this reform a month before simply let it occur.

Finally, in 2007, a reform bill to take the tax from a one-time slam to a rate of a dollar per week passed the General Assembly and Governor Rendell signed the bill. Those who reasonably expected to earn less than $12,000 annually were finally exempted in time for 2008. That shouldn't have taken three years, but the Harrisburg power structure is always more interested in accommodating men in suits than it is doing meat-and-potatoes work that might bring some measure of fairness to the working class. The same post-election session that denied this reform in 2006 saw America's Most Expensive Legislature rush through a bill to allow casinos to ply patrons with free drinks.

This fiasco exemplifies a state that has made its jobs centers the enemy, pitting neighboring communities against each other. The media, of course, invariably describes any restructuring as a "state bailout," a description that city residents find hilarious. They are paying more than ever. In addition to the full $52, the state also mandated that working city residents needed to pay more of their 3 percent wage taxes to the city and less to the public schools. Meantime, the parking tax—largely paid by commuters—would decrease gradually from 50 percent in 2006 to 35 percent in 2010.

That parking tax tango typifies our whacked-out metropolitan split. Private garages haven't been cutting rates as the tax goes down. Why would they? With state policy encouraging everyone to move to the sub-urbs, tens of thousands of commuters drive to the city each workday one to a car, taking all available spaces, making each space dear. Until God repeals the law of supply and demand, parking magnates will continue to charge whatever they can get. A high parking tax is counterproductive because it gives suburbanites another reason to curse a strapped city and stay home, but the real problem is the counterproductive structure of our metropolitan area.

There is little comfort in knowing we're not the only freakishly small American city sputtering for air, even as an unusually high number of the region's workers earn a paycheck within Pittsburgh's borders. According to the Brookings Institution, only twenty-nine of the one hundred larg-est metro areas have a higher percentage of jobs in the urban core than Pittsburgh.[16]

I once thought Pittsburgh might have a model for success in Boston.

More than a century older than Pittsburgh, Beantown knows the headaches of decaying infrastructure, high pension costs and the rest. It takes up even less room on the map, too, squeezing more than five hundred fifty thousand people into less than forty-nine square miles. Its high cost of living makes it more a city of renters than homeowners, and it has much more immigration, but, like Pittsburgh, about six of every ten housing structures were built before 1940. Its role in the regional economy is similar, too. Boston's leading industries are education, health and social services, and Pittsburgh has even more of its future riding on those horses.

That means both these places have leading employers sitting on tax-exempt land, but when I looked up the Boston budget, I found the city expected $404 million in state aid from Massachusetts in 2004. Though state aid was down considerably, it remained Boston's second largest revenue source after property taxes. Boston also gets about five times as much payment in lieu of taxes from its nonprofit groups as Pittsburgh does. The enormous endowments of Harvard and the Massachusetts Institute of Technology may make Boston unique, but Pitt's endowment stood around two billion dollars in 2008, Carnegie Mellon's topped one billion dollars, and you already know of UPMC's wealth. The city shouldn't have to beg for revenue.

Massachusetts shared more than $5 billion in state revenue with its municipalities in a recent year. They can do that with a state income tax considerably higher than Pennsylvania's (5.3 percent to 3.07 percent). That's not to say we should raise income taxes, but what of New England's acknowledgment that most doctors and professors paying beaucoup bucks in state taxes are probably making their money in city hospitals and universities? There should be some payback.

When it comes to Pittsburgh and Boston, we're talking apples and oranges, or maybe wedding soup and chowder. San Francisco is another small-on-the-map city that does big things, but this isn't California any more than it is Massachusetts. As James Carville once described Pennsylvania, we're Philadelphia and Pittsburgh with Alabama in between. Folks don't cotton to change.

Whether you prefer the blue-state model of Massachusetts or some twist on the red-state models mentioned earlier, it's clear we Pennsylvanians are treating cities in ways almost nobody else does anymore, if they ever did. There are no good models for our bassackwards political system, where it pays not to provide any family-sustaining jobs in your community, but rather to keep them in the city next door.

In 2007, State Representative Bob Freeman, a Democrat from Easton, grew tired of seeing all the state's cities imploding while they hosted their region's job centers. Representative Freeman suggested directing the revenue from the state's 18 percent tax on wine and liquor toward those communities that have high levels of tax-exempt land. As I write, that redirection of state funds has not been approved, but if something like that doesn't happen soon, perhaps Allegheny County, not the city, should be running this metropolis.

All of this invites the obvious question: If the system is so obviously broken, why don't we fix it?

Never discount the power of inertia. Even you, a person who cares enough about Pittsburgh to have opened this book, likely prefers I get back to those stories where beer was involved. We all thirst for easy answers in this life. The last thing anyone wants to do when he or she gets home after a hard day's work is to think about public policy. Many would rather watch that show where women in tank tops eat bugs, or bad singers get insulted by an egomaniacal Brit, or maybe catch the reruns of *America's Funniest Groin Injuries*.

Our natural inertia is fed, too, by ignorance. Local media feed the myth that most problems are confined to the city, while any comprehensive look at Allegheny County shows that we're operating under a Darwinian model. Only it's not survival of the fittest; it's survival of the newest.

If property taxes are low in your township, it's not likely because the government is more efficient than the one next door. Nor does the size of the community have a great deal to do with it. The three biggest determinants of low real estate taxes are:

1. A recent housing boom on previously fallow land,
2. Zoning that mostly excludes poor folks, and
3. Few jobs within your borders (unless they're at a mall or an airport).

The closer a municipality comes to these guideposts, the more likely it will have a low tax rate. To put that another way, if your hometown ever had a steel mill and lost it, you're cooked. If the federal or state government just spent hundreds of millions building an airport or a highway nearby, you're doing great—provided you had the empty acres to convert to malls or high-end homes.

There are exceptions, but that's pretty much the story. If your boom came in the '80s and '90s, you're benefiting from a time when many of your residents are in their prime earning years. Big modern homes mean the tax rate doesn't have to be that high to rake in a bundle.

If your boom came from the 1950s through the 1970s, you're probably still OK, though places such as Penn Hills and Pleasant Hills have begun to feel the pinch of health care costs and sewage repair. They were among more than a dozen suburbs that raised their municipal real estate tax rate at least one mill in 2004. (A mill equals a dollar for every thousand dollars in property value.) Those tax hikes affected more than 120,000 people and amounted to millions of dollars, and, barring a shift in where young families move, that trend will only get worse in the inner suburbs as the population ages. This demographic phenomenon just hasn't gotten the attention it deserves because our media don't devote nearly as much time to the county's other one hundred twenty-nine communities as they do to the big ol' one in the middle.

Outlying counties are no different. A University of Pittsburgh study in 2008 suggested that 80 percent of the region's 553 cities, boroughs and towns had budget deficits at least once between 2000 and 2005.

Anyone who deviates from the talk-show story line in this way runs the risk of being called an apologist for the city. But ignoring the context of Western Pennsylvania's problem makes one an apologist for the state. Pennsylvania has no strong cities. How can that be ignored?

Rotting from within is not just a problem for Pittsburghers. People are not just moving from the city, after all. They are leaving the county, the region and the state, and precious few people have moved here to take their places.

Within a few weeks of the announcement in 2007 that the *Places Rated Almanac* had once again named the Pittsburgh metro area as "America's Most Livable City," the Brookings Institution ranked the city 254th on economic conditions and 250th on residential well-being. That's among 302 cities.

The thinkers at Brookings believe there's a way to restore prosperity to America's older cities, however.

"To be sure, Pittsburgh has a wide range of attributes and resources— affordable, walkable neighborhoods, reasonable commute times, historic buildings, a slew of recreational amenities—that make it a good place in which to buy a home and raise a family," wrote Bruce Katz and Jennifer Vey of Brookings in the *Post-Gazette*'s Forum Section in May 2007, making me wonder if they were coming out with a book of their own.

"But these assets haven't been enough to keep and attract residents and jobs. At least not yet."

They like that this region has nearly two dozen four-year and two-year colleges and universities, and nearly twenty hospitals and medical facilities. They give Pennsylvania more credit than I would for some reinvestment in the older cities and towns. But they don't see a true reform agenda.

Pittsburgh and every other struggling Pennsylvania community (that would be most of them) "need more latitude and support to collaborate across the arcane labyrinth of municipal boundaries that, aside from being absurdly inefficient, also undercut the competitiveness of the entire state," Katz and Vey wrote. "With hundreds of counties, cities, boroughs and townships competing for businesses and jobs, they all engage in a race to the bottom that no one can possibly win . . . ."

Hundreds? Actually, there are 2,566 municipalities in Pennsylvania. What those of us who live in and among these relics really need is an exciting way to change things. Nobody is going to carry the water when the call to arms goes this way:

Local leaders now need to urge the General Assembly to enact the legal changes necessary to facilitate the consolidation of the city and county governments and to provide incentives for voluntary collaboration among local governments.

You don't lead a cavalry charge by yelling "facilitate!" I'd put it this way. We in Pennsylvania have to do what cities in the red states have done. We can either give people more reasons to choose to live in the urban cores (expensive gasoline may do some of that arguing for us). Or we can make that choice less relevant. We don't need the city to annex the suburbs. But if The Pittsburgh Promise fails to stem the city's bleeding, or if there's no move to compensate the communities that host all the tax-exempt property, we may need the suburbs to take ownership of the city by melding the city into Allegheny County, and have all county residents be able to vote on the metropolitan issues that affect them. The devil would be in the grim details of the city's massive debt, but this oversight stuff is a halfway measure. So are joint city-county purchasing agreements. Why not go all the way?

I'm afraid there's a long answer to that, too. Late in 2007, I went to see David Rusk, the former Albuquerque mayor who has written and lectured widely about the advantages "flexible cities" have by annexing suburbs. Rusk gave the keynote address to the fourth annual Equitable Development Summit at Pittsburgh's Twentieth Century Club. (The city could use a Twenty-first Century Club.)

Nothing about that fourth annual summit made me sorry I'd missed the first three, but Rusk did jolt the crowd by saying there's no way Pittsburgh and Allegheny County can ever combine. The state won't formally merge municipalities, and local voters will never vote for meaningful mergers. As for city-county consolidation, forget it.

"It's a worthless concept here," Rusk said. "It would have no value here."

Every inch of Allegheny County is already spoken for. The county has no dowry of unincorporated land to bring to a marriage with the city; it's entirely taken by its one hundred thirty municipalities. In every other American city that consolidated with the surrounding county, the city merged only with the unincorporated parts of the county. Incorporated municipalities retain their independence—and every place in Allegheny County is incorporated.

Some there cheered Rusk because they fear the city getting hosed even further if its voting power is diluted. Others wanted to wash Rusk's mouth out with position papers. Brian Jensen, the Allegheny Conference vice president in charge of fretting over local governments, said Rusk's view is too limited. The idea is to have one captain at the helm. Instead of a mayor and a county chief executive, have one person in charge. That only makes sense, Jensen believes, and likely would make the area more attractive to companies looking to grow. There also would be ways to save money by moving toward one county police force, having the county run the big city parks, and so forth.

By April 2008, the 250th anniversary of the establishment of Fort Pitt, Pittsburgh's leaders were on board. Allegheny County Executive Dan Onorato and his fellow North Catholic alum, Pittsburgh Mayor Luke Ravenstahl, endorsed the concept of merging city and county. Onorato had been heading in that direction for some time.

"There's no reason why the city and county [can't] end up as one government one day, and you have a mayor of Greater Pittsburgh," Onorato said early in 2007. "You can leave the municipalities alone. You can leave the school districts alone. . . . We both have public works. We both have parks and recreation. We both have a department of engineering . . . there's no reason you can't run those departments out of one office.

"The eight hundred-pound gorilla in the room of that [city-county] merger debate is the unfunded pension and debt service in the city," Onorato said.

There's no way to fix that without going to the state. Onorato most definitely does not expect the county majority in the suburbs to step up and say, "Oh, we'll take that." He thinks we'd need new state law for a referendum.

"It would be a package and the idea would be, 'Hey, state, you have to help fix the unfunded pension and the outstanding debt, and in return, you'd get efficiencies.'" The state legislature has no interest in taking this on, but Onorato aspires to be governor. Maybe he'll find a way to make it work if he gets the job, but that's going to be a tough sell in the hinterlands.

Mayor Luke Ravenstahl, who at twenty-six became the youngest big-city mayor in America after the death of Bob O'Connor in 2006, added another wrinkle.

"It doesn't make any sense for us to relinquish our assets—and we do have great assets—while still left dealing with our debt and legacy costs," Ravenstahl told the *PG* a few months before he easily beat back a Republican challenge for his job.

In that mayor's race of November 2007, I voted for the challenger, Mark DeSantis. He was the most well-funded Republican candidate in almost four decades and he benefited from an avalanche of bad press that fell on Ravenstahl in the months prior to the election, all of which meant diddly. DeSantis got just 35 percent of the vote.

This book is unapologetically light on what mayors have done in Pittsburgh because they're generally less interesting than the people who elect them, and they haven't the power to fix the real problem anyway. I voted for DeSantis, not because I thought he or his party necessarily had better answers, but because Republicans have to get in the urban game.

Bedroom communities are easier to run than cities, for all the reasons previously cited. Until Republicans run a big city, an entirely different organism in a metropolitan ecosystem, they won't understand, or at least won't say out loud, that the cities of Pennsylvania are designed to fail. The tax base isn't there and the hyper-fragmentation of governments encourages Pennsylvanians to live outside the cities, absent special incentives such as The Pittsburgh Promise.

It's pretty clear that one-party rule in Pittsburgh is no laboratory for innovation. The city hasn't known a time when the mayor's chair is genuinely in play between the two major parties since at least the nineteenth century, if it happened then. We had an entrenched, corrupt Republican machine before the Democratic machine took over with the New Deal in the early 1930s and began playing the same patronage games. The last time a Republican candidate got more than 40 percent of the vote was 1945. Most people in the city register Democratic not just because that's how they lean, but because the Democratic primary is the only election that means anything.

Republican leaders care less about this than they let on. They pay no political penalty for the Democrats being unable to figure out how to balance a budget without a tax base. To the contrary, they reap the political dividends when taxpayers flee to the suburbs. Republicans don't seem to care overmuch that a lot of Pennsylvanians flee the state entirely because those who stay wind up strengthening the GOP base in the suburbs. Why screw that up?

Bill Green, a Republican consultant, came about as close as anyone has come to acknowledging that implicit strategy after DeSantis's defeat.

"My belief is that you should just cede the city to the Democratic Party and work in the county where the Republican Party has an opportunity to grow and expand," Green told the *Post-Gazette*. "Trying to do anything in the city, above winning a City Council seat or two, is quixotic, at best.

"I know I sound awfully pessimistic, but I'm not," Green continued. "I'm being realistic. There have been leadership gaps in the Republican Party here, and the statewide party focuses on winning county elections and neglects the inner cities."

"The Democrats have controlled this city. They've put it into bankruptcy. I've advised Republicans over the years, 'Why would you even want to be mayor of this city?' Let the Democrats who created this mess fix it."

An anti-city stance is enormously popular with suburban constituents. That's not great statecraft, but it is great politics.

People who don't believe Pittsburgh's problem lies as much in Harrisburg as it does on Grant Street, who don't see how out of sync Pennsylvania's fixed municipal boundaries are with the growing cities of America, should consider this: In 2000, the year of the last U.S. Census, Pittsburgh was still more densely populated than five of the ten largest cities in the United States. Strange as that may sound, there were more people per square mile in the city that had misplaced half its population than in Houston, Phoenix, San Diego, Dallas or San Antonio. They aren't cities in the way we in the Northeast know them. None of these Sun Belt cities has even 4,000 people per square mile, and the average is closer to 3,000. They're closer in size and texture to Allegheny County (about 1,750 people per square mile in 2006) than to the shrinking city in its belly (about 5,600 the same year).

It's ironic that suburban Republicans have been the most resistant to the arguments to consolidate city and county, because the models all favor them. The five biggest Sun Belt cities went for President Bush in 2004, a detail particularly noteworthy when one considers that he took only nine

Population Per Sq. Mi. for the Ten Most Populous Cities				
1910			**2000**	
New York	16,621	1	New York	26,404
Chicago	11,806	2	Los Angeles	7,876
Philadelphia	11,897	3	Chicago	12,752
St. Louis	11,189	4	Houston	3,372
Boston	16,316	5	Philadelphia	11,233
Cleveland	12,295	6	Phoenix	2,782
Baltimore	18,554	7	San Diego	3,772
Pittsburgh	12,896	8	Dallas	3,470
Detroit	11,416	9	San Antonio	2,808
Buffalo	10,949	10	Detroit	6,854
		53	Pittsburgh	6,017

counties with populations above one million. John Kerry took twenty-five. It is a rule of thumb that the closer people live to one another, the more likely they are to vote Democratic. Reasons can be argued into the night, but if suburbanites and city residents are to unite, as the numbers suggest they should, they will have to remember the other rule in politics: No one gives up power without a fight. Allegheny County presents unique challenges in that regard, at least one hundred thirty of them. That's the number of municipalities within the County. (See map on page 10).

Pittsburgh: You're My Density

Pittsburgh, as I said, with less than half as many people per square mile as it had in 1910, still had more than twice as many folks per square mile as San Antonio and Phoenix, and 60 to 78 percent more than San Diego, Dallas and Houston. New York and Chicago, packed tighter than ever, are the exceptions among American cities, not the rule.

This is what Pittsburgh might look like had it played the same game as these southwestern cities and annexed the surrounding area for the past half-century or so.

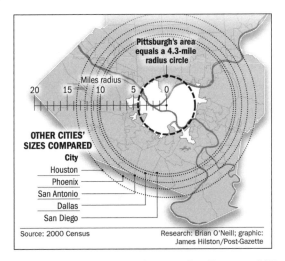

Footprints that Dallas, Houston, San Antonio, San Diego and Phoenix would have in Allegheny County.

The smallest of these cities, San Diego, would swallow about 90 of Allegheny County's 130 municipalities whole and take pieces of more than a dozen others. The northern line would split Hampton and McCandless; the southern line would go deep into Upper St. Clair and Bethel Park;

the eastern boundary would cut through Penn Hills and Monroeville and the western one would slice Moon.

More than 900,000 "Pittsburghers" live within that circle, by my guess.

The largest city in the Sun Belt quintet, Houston, would stretch wide enough to touch all but a dozen communities in Allegheny County, and would get into Peters in Washington County. About 1.2 million people live within that circle.

These are approximations. There's no need to be precise. Cities don't grow in perfect circles. The population of any of these circles, however, would make Pittsburgh the ninth largest city in the country.

Fractured Fairy Tale

There are more municipalities in Allegheny County than in Montana, a state two hundred times the county's land area. Ponder that. While Montana might not catch up to our county in population for another couple of decades, what are we doing with more towns and cities than the fourth most spacious state?

Our set-up makes it "rational to do the irrational," says John A. Powell of Ohio State University, who has studied us closely. "It's rational not to ever cooperate, to rob your neighbor."

We have enough police departments in this county for the chiefs alone to form a ten-team softball league and still leave bench strength. They don't have that softball league, as far as I know, but that could be a project for the county police chiefs association. We have one of those.

Hundreds of borderlines can make any crime a nightmare of buck-passing if the thief has the audacity to wander a few miles, or even a few blocks, during his spree.

Wayne Jones, a Dormont resident who works in the city, lost his check-book in Parkway Center Mall in the summer of 2002, and someone later used it to write a bad check at a flea market off I-79 south of the city. So far, so bad, and it gets worse.

"The Dormont police told us to call the city police since that's where the theft took place," Jones recalled.

Dormont police were correct, mind you. Parkway Center is within the city limits. But when city police took Jones' report, he was told to call back the Dormont police so they could "shepherd" all the bad checks that might come in. The city also told Jones to call the police department with juris-diction at the flea market.

Dormont police did not agree with city police about this shepherding business. Jones was told once again Dormont had no horse in this race. So Jones tried finding which police department had jurisdiction. The first municipal office he called near the flea market didn't even have a police department, and directed him to the South Fayette police. When he called there, Jones was told to get a copy of the Pittsburgh police report because the city allegedly "doesn't like to share those." So Jones had to go Downtown to buy the kind of paperwork that a grown-up metropolis would have in one place.

"Tear down the walls!" Jones said.

The crooks were eventually caught at a flea market in North Versailles. A husband and wife team was charged with multiple counts for eleven bad checks. They'd been hitting bingo halls, too. Almost every check was written in a different municipality.

That's not surprising. Fifty municipalities in this county take up less than a square mile. Sixteen have fewer than one thousand residents. Seventy have fewer than five thousand. More than one hundred places have fewer than the ten thousand people who might drop by the U.S. Steel Tower come Monday. The Waterfront shopping complex alone covers three municipalities. An ambitious crook could write bad checks in Homestead, West Homestead and Munhall before he got back to his car.

This kind of fragmentation brings a special frustration to police dispatchers. A couple of years ago, a 911 operator told me about the difficulty of catching people who drink and drive on Route 65.

"Try taking a call from someone following a drunk driver who starts in Bellevue and is heading north on 65," she said. "They can pass through eight different towns in less than a few miles.

"There are daily calls from people on cell phones who are involved in road-rage incidents or following intoxicated drivers and our job is hampered due to all these municipalities. Many of these driving dialers cross several town lines while talking to the dispatcher, which means they can be transferred to other agencies and sometimes back again."

Thus do drunk and raging drivers get away. Dispatchers then ask callers if they want to pull over and make a report. Most don't.

"The call that caused a lot of work for the caller, police and dispatcher was useless due to these tiny municipalities that someone on a cell phone can drive through in the blink of an eye."

Given more than one hundred police departments (most of which don't even have ten cops), more than two hundred fire departments and seventy emergency medical services units, dispatchers are remarkably adept.

Dispatchers taking calls from Route 65 and roads like it have learned to ask for landmarks, such as gas stations, rather than ask what town the cell phone user thinks he is in. He might be wrong before he finishes his answer.

When I called Bob Harvey, the county's 911 manager, a few years ago he was a good soldier and downplayed the difficulties. But he also said he'd looked for a peer in another county in America that is split one hundred thirty ways and "can't find anybody like that."

Of course, he can't. When the U.S. Census Bureau took a look at the twenty-five largest metropolitan areas a few years ago, it found 418 local governments in the six-county Pittsburgh region. That worked out to 17.7 governments per one hundred thousand residents. No metropolis in America comes close. Minneapolis, St. Louis and Cincinnati deal with around twelve governments per one hundred thousand people, and even they are way out of step with the nation.

The median is Portland, Oregon, with 4.1 governments per one hundred thousand people. The average is between five and six. Residents of the Pittsburgh region pay three to four times as many chiefs as most places. This only seems normal because we live in Pennsylvania. Of the state's 2,566 municipalities, four of every five have fewer than five thousand residents.

Amoebas split less often.

Nobody designing a county for the twenty-first century would set one up our way. Nearly everyone concedes that. Our governmental structure is way past the sell-by-date, a leftover from the nineteenth century. Back then, small, relatively independent economies were centered in mill towns and farming communities. Most Allegheny County municipalities sprouted after the Civil War, with a third of them coming into being between 1891 and 1910. Private entrepreneurs drew lines around their mills and factories because they wanted to make their own rules, and to employ their own cops to help keep the unions down.[17]

This was also a time when immigration was high, so part of the rationale for hyper-fragmentation was to accommodate the prejudices of the time.

Around the lowland mills crowded the immigrants, the Slavs, the Germans, the Italians, and the Irish with their tolerance for saloons and their devotion to the Roman Catholic Church. On the hills lived the

Presbyterians with their abhorrence for alcohol and their dedication to Protestantism.[18]

That's history. Nearly all the mills are gone and, everything being relative, we have a more mixed society. But the boundaries erected to suit the economy of the nineteenth century have remained, even if they no longer make sense.

The only place left in the county where people mostly work where they live is Pittsburgh itself. More than 80 percent of city residents who earn a paycheck do so without leaving town. The only other place where even a third of the workers stay put is McKeesport. In just a dozen other places do even a fifth of the workers work where they live. The Rand Corporation recently found that, on average, only 13 percent of county residents work where they live.[19]

"For one hundred fourteen of the one hundred thirty municipalities," wrote Sally Sleeper of Rand, "eighty cents of every dollar earned comes from other locales." Pittsburgh is the region's economic engine, kicking out more than 30 percent of earnings in about half the county's municipalities.

There just aren't any self-sustaining places in Allegheny County, and haven't been for at least two generations. The city needs commuters and commuters need the city. Period.

So why is the city still the jobs center if it's doing everything wrong? How come the next ten municipalities combined don't approach the number of jobs within the city limits? Why is one of every four jobs in the region within three miles of the Point? Why did a city that lost population in the 1990s actually have more people earning a paycheck within its borders at the decade's end? Why does a city of three hundred thousand-plus grow by another one hundred thirty-eight thousand each working day?[20]

It's not just the central location. Luminaries in the Hole in the Donut School of Economics dream of a day when everyone drives to jobs in the hinterlands. So do oil sheiks. But these folks miss a key reason why, for example, the banking centers and hospitals have thrived in the city: Pittsburgh has the most people ready to work for low pay.

Those who know their way around a luxury box don't much think about that because the city also has the most jobs with high pay, but the median household income in Allegheny County was around $41,000 in 2003. If we excluded Pittsburgh, that figure would be even higher because the city's median household income didn't reach $31,000. A large percentage of these folks are retirees, but many more clean, cook, copy, cashier, sing, guard, nurse, repair, act, park, type, wash dishes, tend phones, tend bar, wait tables and make coffee for everyone else. They're the glue. They're why most of the region's work is done in the city, and they've been paying 3 percent of their wages to the city and schools to keep the machine running.

Others, of course, have fled to the suburbs to dodge the tax. That move is not only entirely rational; it is what Pennsylvania has encouraged. It doesn't seem like a sustainable strategy for the long haul, but it is what we have.

Our plan seems to be: Pretend we're not a metropolitan area until it goes away.

Kilbuck Loses in a Landslide

Dirt, rock and trees covered a closed Route 65 in Kilbuck Township beginning in September 2006. Darrell Sapp, Pittsburgh Post-Gazette.

One recurring argument for our hyper-fragmentation is that most people like it this way, but when have we been given another choice? Russell Hardiman tried to get his Kilbuck neighbors a better arrangement, but no longer has much chance to turn a township of seven hundred souls into a neighborhood of the same. You might say he lost in a landslide.

Hardiman campaigned to become a Kilbuck supervisor in 2003, arguing that the community should merge with neighboring Ohio Township. He narrowly won his write-in campaign, 135 to 128. Since then, Hardiman often has felt like the John Belushi character in *Animal House*. You know that scene where Belushi gives an impassioned speech and then yells "Who's with me?!"?

Nobody follows him when he runs out the door.

Hardiman did get the Governor's Center for Local Government Services to study the potential consolidation of the two townships, but he was the only one of three Kilbuck supervisors to support it. The governor's big thinkers returned a study that said, yes, the townships should be combined but no, not now.

Both Ohio and Kilbuck townships have good homes with residents of above-average educations and incomes. They share a school district. Both are small with growth potential. What's not to merge?

Whatever chance Hardiman had of making that case ended in September 2006 when a good bit of Kilbuck slid into the middle of Route 65. That four-lane road generally carries twenty-two thousand commuters but can't when five hundred thousand cubic yards of rocks and dirt block the way. The landslide came after the township, desperate to expand its tiny tax base, relaxed its grading requirements in 2002 so a Super Wal-Mart complex could squeeze in. Pennsylvania being Pennsylvania, almost none of the commuters and merchants affected by that decision could do a thing about it because they weren't among the seven hundred souls who live in Kilbuck. All hell didn't have to break loose before Pennsylvania stepped in to halt construction; all hill did the trick.

Ohio Township had turned down that Wal-Mart more than once, and it wasn't an amicable breakup even before the superstore's dirt hit the road. Ohio Township ultimately tossed a big tax break Target's way, and the county and Avonworth School District did the same, but that superstore managed to build on its hill without tumbling down to the Parkway North, which was appreciated.

I have genuine sympathy for the residents of Kilbuck. They would not have created this mess had Pennsylvania not set "every municipality for itself" as our fundamental rule. Kilbuck supervisors had worked hard to lower property taxes, taking drastic measures such as closing the ironically named Harmony Road that runs through the township but was used mostly by Ohio Township residents. Like so much around here, that road was crumbling, and the neighboring communities were perfectly happy to keep that Kilbuck's problem (every municipality for itself). So the road became a roadblock; Harmony Road closed early in 2006, indefinitely and perhaps permanently, with the little township unable to come up with the millions of dollars it would take to fix it. Then came the landslide, making Hardiman something of a prophet, because he had told me in 2004, "We're a disaster away from double-digit [property tax] millage again."

Not many Western Pennsylvanians want to face this. Hardiman remembers a call in 2004 from a resident of neighboring Ben Avon Heights, complaining that Kilbuck needed to fix its part of Ben Avon Heights Road. A man from one of the most prosperous, lowest taxed parts of the county was telling a representative of a highly taxed place what to do with money he didn't have.

We should make T-shirts: "Pittsburgh: We Keep Doing What Doesn't Work Because We Always Have."

Hardiman envisions a future where Emsworth, Kilbuck, Ben Avon, Ben Avon Heights and Ohio Township all merge and pool their resources. That kind of thinking could one day get this county down from 130 municipalities to 43, which is how many school districts we have scattered hereabouts. Allegheny County Executive Dan Onorato has floated that trial balloon but it hasn't gone anywhere.

You'd think the illogic of the fragmented map of Pennsylvania, the apparent work of a quilting bee on speed, might one day prompt the State Legislature to give localities the tools and incentives to merge, in the way so many businesses have done. But even if that happens, a long shot given the fat and happy nature of the 253-member Legislature itself, we can't be sure that logic will carry the day.

I witnessed that special Pennsylvanian pride in inertia in the mid-'90s when the 853 people in Wall danced with the idea of merging with the 2,222 people of Wilmerding. Folks in Wilmerding got cold feet. Emotions can win out over reason when municipalities start cuddling. One Wall resident told me in 1995, "I don't want to go to Wilmerding for a measly 40 percent [drop in property taxes]."

Until then, I'd never heard the word "measly" in front of "40 percent drop in taxes." Clearly, it will take more than reason; it will take emotion for reformers to win.

The possibility of a Kilbuck-Ohio merger probably died the day that hillside lost its battle with gravity. Wal-Mart ended its five-and-a-half year struggle with physics and foes late in 2007 when it announced it would return the hillside to its natural state. It's hardly coincidence that, soon after, Kilbuck supervisors decided the township hadn't the money to keep its police force of two full-time and seven part-time officers. State police filled the immediate gap, and by the following spring Ohio Township had been contracted to provide police, making Kilbuck the seventh community Ohio patrols in addition to the home turf. Kilbuck police had a reputation for writing traffic tickets to Route 65 motorists to cover its budget, so not everyone mourned the loss of the little department.

In 2008, Kilbuck caught a break by contracting with neighboring Avalon to have its borough manager administer Kilbuck as well. But why should these catch-as-catch-can deals be as far as municipal mergers go? The questions Hardiman asked his neighbors before Wal-Mart hit the skids would be similar in a thousand locations.

"What truly changes if Kilbuck becomes part of Ohio township?" Hardiman asked. "When we wake up in the morning, we'll still live in the same houses. We'll drive the same roads. We'll have the same neighbors. Our kids will go to the exact same schools. We'll shop at the same stores, go to the same churches. There will be only two differences: the name of the township and the amount of taxes we pay.

"Frankly, if it lowers my taxes, I don't care what you call it. Call it the Cleveland Browns Township."

He needs to work on that speech some.

The Whitest Large Metro Area in the Country

More European than some cities in Europe: Father Gervase Degenhart, a parochial vicar at St. Augustine's Catholic Church in Lawrenceville, tends to his roses in 2002. Robin Rombach, Pittsburgh Post-Gazette.

It's no accident that Pittsburgh escapes mention in David Brooks' 2004 book, *On Paradise Drive: How We Live Now (And Always Have) in the Future Tense.*

"When you go to a country where the past is more real than the future, and then you return to America," Brooks wrote, "it becomes clear how distinct the American imagination really is, and how each of us in this culture is molded by our horizon dreams."

Horizon dreams? I don't need a passport to see a place where the past seems more real than the future. I live in Pittsburgh. What I see coming over the horizon is another guy wearing a Jack Lambert jersey.

For all our surface toughness, we're timid hereabouts. We're old. We're settled. We don't have many people coming here from somewhere else. You know that theory of six degrees of separation that says everyone on Earth is just six people removed from knowing everyone else. Adam Meyer, who grew up on the North Side and went to Pitt, says we've refined that here.

"In Pittsburgh," Meyer says, "you're five people away from being a cousin."

How deep are the roots? Among the forty-six metropolitan areas with more than a million residents, Pittsburgh had the highest percentage of people who had lived in the same house since 1959. Some 19 percent of our people haven't moved since Eisenhower was in the White House.

Such steadfastness makes us more European than most American cities. One can even argue that we are more European than most European cities, given their heavy immigration from Africa and Asia. Looking at our ten-county area, more than 97 percent of southwestern Pennsylvanians were born in the United States, and more than 90 percent are white. Among the 2.6 million residents, only sixty-six thousand residents are foreign born, and almost half of them were born in Europe. Among the 5 percent of the population who spoke a language other than English at home in the year 2000, that language was likely to be something other than Spanish or an Asian language.[21] We've quite literally missed the boat (and the planes and the vans) on a huge American trend.

I went into Mullaney's Harp and Fiddle in the Strip District for a pint early one evening a few years ago, seeking just sixteen ounces of put-the-day-behind-me before riding the 54C home. Behind the bar was that rarest of Pittsburgh creatures, an immigrant.

Declan Gilbert, formerly of Cork on Ireland's south coast, has tended bar in Mullaney's since it opened in 1992, and Pittsburgh is the better for it. Gilbert met his wife, Darcy Thull in Mullaney's, a place that counts more than thirty couples who married after meeting at the pub, if you're looking. So this Irishman, now an American father, seems here to stay. Such a tale is rare in Pittsburgh.

America's largest one hundred cities added a total of 4.7 million people in the 1990s, according to CEOs for Cities.

"Seventy-five percent of that growth, or 3.5 million people, was due to the growth in the foreign-born population," CEOs for Cities reported. "The average growth in foreign-born population among the largest one hundred cities was a stunning eighty-three percent, while the average growth in native-born population was only four percent."[22]

Our city trailed the field badly, gaining 11 percent in foreign-born residents, while both blacks and whites left. Such a small bump in immigrants still left us looking less like a modern American metropolis than the earlier, European-American kind that Damon Runyon wrote about in *Guys and Dolls*. A number of years ago, I went to a prizefight featuring Paul Spadafora of McKees Rocks and, after joining the partisan crowd of Irish- and German-and Polish-and Italian-Americans chanting "Spad-DEE, Spad-DEE," it occurred to me I had stumbled into a scene from my old man's life in the 1930s.

That could happen only in Pittsburgh. If we don't count Latinos, whites are now a minority of the combined population of America's one hundred largest cities. Nearly half the cities are home to more blacks, Hispanics, Asians and other minorities than whites.

In other words, what we've had in Pittsburgh for the past fifty years, middle-class whites heading for the suburbs, is in no way unusual. If anything, the movement has been restrained. That nationwide trend in the 1990s saw seventy-one of the top one hundred American cities losing white residents. What's abnormal is our not getting our fair share of immigrants, and not becoming more diverse. That's what separates us from the rest of America. That and holding fast to our buggy-age boundaries.

As it happens, I had a revelation that night in Mullaney's. I fell into conversation with a thoughtful gent on the next stool, with the kind of philosophizing for which God created pubs. It's possible a six o'clock news story on the TV screen sparked it. I don't recall. But the man began remarking on the region's woeful lack of immigration and I thought, my God, a progressive in our midst.

The barstool sociologist went on to suggest that Pittsburgh ought consciously to lure Eastern Europeans here because we already had the infrastructure of churches, social clubs and history in place. And I thought, mister, you're not missing the boat. You're missing the plane. And the van.

I need to be clear here. I have nothing against Eastern Europeans. We should welcome everyone, by all means, and I happen to be one-eighth Eastern European myself. My paternal great-grandmother was Polish.

(My dad's side of the family began boasting of this at roughly the moment Pope John Paul II was introduced to the crowd in St. Peter's Square.) But in 2004, when I asked readers for new slogans for our beleaguered city, Emmett and Christine Smith, then of the North Side, nailed us with "Pittsburgh: Where integrated means wedding soup AND pierogies."

This is a town where even progressive thinkers leaven their ideas with nods to centuries past. That's part of what I love about Pittsburgh, but we should manage an occasional look around America on our way to yet another gaze backward into Pittsburgh's past. In an era when Latinos have become the largest minority group in America, here they've been largely invisible apart from the Roberto Clemente statue outside PNC Park.

It's possible that's finally changing, in the way things so often do in Pittsburgh, a decade or more behind the rest of America. In December 2007, a mariachi band played on the steps of St. Paul Cathedral before a Mass celebrating the feast of Our Lady of Guadalupe, the Mexican icon, and more than a thousand people attended. I took that as a good sign.

On the other hand, census takers in 2000 managed to find only 11,166 Latinos in a county of nearly 1.3 million. That's less than 1 percent, a ratio that isn't much higher in the city. From 2000 to 2006, less than sixteen thousand international immigrants moved to the Pittsburgh area, which put the region last among America's twenty-five largest metro areas. Despite that, local politicians such as Representative Daryl Metcalfe of Cranberry can still make political hay with hyperbolic cries of "an illegal alien invasion." That became a big issue in Western Pennsylvania in 2007 for reasons hard to fathom, but it probably has something to do with a general sense of declining fortunes.

We need Latinos. We need more than the 21,716 Asians who represented less than 2 percent of the county population in 2000. We need anyone and everyone, but when Latinos and Asians arrive in great numbers, that likely will be the signal that Pittsburgh has regained its stature. Don't expect us to rebound without 'em.

The Deer People

One winter, a decade or so back, I woke before dawn to drive fifty miles south on Interstate 79 to meet a nun with a gun. An hour or so later, Sister Mary Joy Haywood spontaneously fired her .243 rifle to get the last shell out before we headed up for a deer stand, and I made silent thanks that I hadn't taken up her mother's offer of prunes that morning.

It might seem odd to wind down a book about Pittsburgh with a story about a shivering man and a gun-toting sister in a Greene County hamlet that's largely pasture punctuated by tree stands, but hang with me. Because I hung with Sister Haywood as Canada geese honked overhead and goose bumps ran up the gap on my calves between my socks and long underwear. Slim and nun, you might have called us. It was getting as cold as a loan officer's heart, and the good sister invited me to go inside and stay warm, but I wasn't about to let a nun out-macho me.

She and I never killed anything more than the time that day. So why do I bring it up? Not because Pennsylvania has nearly a million licensed hunters or because (illegal) deer hunting has taken place within the city limits, though it has. I say it because Pittsburgh is filled with people who act like deer.

Bucks generally travel as juveniles to get some distance from their mother's home range, and then can live out their entire lives in only forty acres if it's good habitat, three hundred acres if it's not. That's also the modus operandi of the average Pittsburgher.

That's me now, too. I may go a shade farther than your average deer, but the days when I go more than a mile and a half from my house are few. I wasn't always such a beast of boredom, but everything I need now seems to be within a short walk or drive from home, right up to salt licks at the watering holes. (Isn't that what the pretzels are for?) This is the way of the Pittsburgher.

We are not entirely like deer. Their population is growing. But this is the capital of No Thanks, I'm Staying Put. The legend that we won't cross rivers may have been put to rest, but we nonetheless stand out in a nation of transients. As I mentioned a few pages back, the census takers say that almost one in five householders in the region has been in the same home for thirty years or more. That tops metro areas of more than one million people, and no other place is close.

Spin that however you like, but whether it's Pittsburgh's inability to attract newcomers or the native desire to stay close to family, we're more like deer than the rest of the country. My friend, Sean Cannon of Shaler, could stand for tens of thousands. One day I mentioned I was going to Pleasant Hills and he asked, "Where's that?"

Cannon has lived in Allegheny County for all of his four decades, and Pleasant Hills is a mere fifteen miles and two rivers away, but it might as well be in Botswana.

"Are you kidding me?" Cannon said. "I only have to travel within a five-mile radius of my home. I have the supermarket, the ball fields, St. Bonaventure, the library and the beer distributor. I'm leading a life of suburban bliss."

He's right. What does it profit a man from the North Hills to explore the southern burbs? It's the same life, different mall. Cannon already has plenty of feed and cover where he is. Contentment is not such a terrible thing, and adventure isn't just about long-distance travel.

But we are more alike than we are different. Somewhere in Pleasant Hills, there's a man who would hold the same indifference for Millvale or Crafton or Bellevue or Sharpsburg. But we all know where the city is, because a part of us still loves it, loves it like a brother who has temporarily lost his way but has plenty of surprises in him yet.

Wherever we go from here, the journey is unlikely to be as painful as the one that got Pittsburgh this far. We need only summon some of that old-time resilience and innovation. The architecture hereabouts, both God's and man's, is very good. Unlike places from Atlanta to Phoenix, we're not short on water.

With worldwide demand for gasoline likely to keep prices high, our relative density will soon be seen as an attribute. With the demographics saying that the U.S. will have as many single-person households as families with children in the next twenty years, a walkable metropolis with high culture and big-time sports begins to look better.

View from the maternity ward of Allegheny General Hospital, North Side, looking toward downtown. Courtesy of Allegheny General Hospital.

Our problems are mundane. Some of the biggest ones are accounting problems. We have to play our cards more wisely. Others may have better, but I still like ours. I wouldn't toss 'em in. Would you?

On the morning our first child was born, I held Curran up to the window high in Allegheny General Hospital, where the Golden Triangle gleamed across the river on a bright, late-winter morning.

I told her, "Girl, that's your city. That's Pittsburgh. Someday this will all be yours."

A nurse laughed and said something like, "I see you have high hopes for her."

She didn't say whether she meant my daughter or Pittsburgh, but in either case, the answer is the same.

I do.

Acknowledgments

I must thank Cheryl Towers and Harold Maguire for their early belief in this book and for helping me shape its structure; *Pittsburgh Post-Gazette* photo editor Jim Mendenhall for encouraging me when the project looked bleakest and for combing the newspaper's computer system for just the right photos; Larry Rippel for the exquisite care he took in finding and shooting the people and places that make this book unique; Ron Donoughe, for creating a cover that inspired me; Peter Leo, Steve Hansen and Grant Oliphant, for telling me I had something to say; to David Shribman, for encouraging me here and in my daily work; to the phenomenal photographers of the *Pittsburgh Post-Gazette* whose photos make this book and every *PG* a visual treat; to Tracy Certo of Pop City, for leading me to the good people at the Carnegie Mellon University Press; to Cynthia Lamb and Shahnaz Islam, for their grace and patience in shepherding this book through 11th-hour revisions; to my neighbors and friends, who finally have an answer to their recurrent question, "Whenzat book coming out?"; and to my wife, Betsy, and our daughters (and contributions to the Pittsburgh census count), Curran and Clare, for giving me the time to write this and the love that gets me out of bed in the morning.

Endnotes

1. (p. 22) Edward L. Glaeser, "Job Sprawl: Employment Location in U.S. Metropolitan Areas," Brookings Institution and Harvard University, Matthew Kahn, Tufts University, and Chenghuan Chu, Stanford University, July 2001, The Brookings Institution Center on Urban & Metropolitan Policy http://www.brookings.edu/es/urban/publications/glaeserjobsprawl.pdf

2. (p. 34) Elwin Green, "Downtown improving but still lags,"*Pittsburgh Post-Gazette,* November 17, 2005.

3. (p. 52) Sam Smith, "Making Cities Black & Poor: The Hidden Story," *The Progressive Review,* January 2000.

4. (p. 54) Mindy Thompson Fullilove, M.D., *Root Shock: How Tearing Up City Neighborhoods Hurts America, And What We Can Do About It* (New York: Ballentine, 2004), 4.

5. (p. 56) Ibid., 61.

6. (p. 65) The Pittsburgh Promise; http://www.pps.k12.pa.us/143110517 15526407/lib/14311051715526407/Why_Pittsburgh_Benefits_from_ The_Promise.PDF

7. (p. 85) Bernard-Henri Levy, "In the Footsteps of Tocqueville" (Part IV) *The Atlantic* (October 2005).

8. (p. 107) Jeff Schlegel, "A Design District Takes Shape," *The New York Times,* October 14, 2007.

9. (p.109) Metropolitan Organization: The Allegheny County Case; U.S. Advisory Commission on Intergovernmental Relations, February 1992, 10.

10. (p. 109) Ibid., 10.

11. (p. 110) Ibid., 10.

12. (p. 110) Ibid., 10.

13. (p. 110) US Census citation in Federal Reserve Bank of St. Louis working paper, "Urban Decentralization and Income Inequality," by Christopher Wheeler, p. 3 2006http://research.stlouisfed.org/wp/2006/2006-037.pdf

14. (p. 113) Edward Robb Ellis, *The Epic of New York City*, 1966, (New York: Coward-McCann), 457.

15. (p. 114) Boundary Change Procedures, [Pennsylvania] Governor's Center for Local Government Services; June 1999, p. 18 www.inventpa.com

16. (p. 117) Edward L. Glaeser, "Job Sprawl: Employment Location in U.S. Metropolitan Areas," Brookings Institution and Harvard University, Matthew Kahn, Tufts University, and Chenghuan Chu, Stanford University, July 2001, The Brookings Institution Center on Urban & Metropolitan Policy http://www.brookings.edu/es/urban/publications/glaeserjobsprawl.pdf

17. (p. 131) Metropolitan Organization: The Allegheny County Case; U.S. Advisory Commission on Intergovernmental Relations, February 1992, 9-10.

18. (p. 132) Ibid., 9-10.

19. (p. 132) "Measuring and Understanding Economic Interdependence in Allegheny County," by Sally Sleeper, Henry Willis, Eric Landree and Beth Grill, Rand Corporation 2004.

20. (p. 132) Mark Roth, "'Day surge' puts 41 percent more people in the city" *Pittsburgh Post-Gazette*, January 16, 2006.

21. (p. 140) Figures from the 2000 United States Census.

22. (p. 141) Robert Weissbourd, "The Changing Dynamics of Urban America," Executive Preview for CEOs for Cities, October 7, 2003, RW Ventures & Christopher Berry, Harvard University, 13.